THE REAL THING

The Real Thing

A guide to separating the genuine from the ersatz, the men from the boys, and the wheat from the chaff.

Kurt Andersen

Doubleday & Company, Inc., Garden City, New York, 1980

Library of Congress Cataloging in Publication Data

Andersen, Kurt, 1954-
The real thing.

I. Title.
PN6162.A54   814'.54
ISBN: 0-385-14636-1
Library of Congress Catalog Card Number 78-22787
Copyright © 1980 by Kurt Andersen
All Rights Reserved
Printed in the United States of America

CONTENTS

INTRODUCTION

I'd best make clear, here at the outset, that *The Real Thing* has no connection with a certain cola-flavored soft drink. If you are among the minority who bought this book with the understanding that it actually contained tiny bottles of soda pop, you now find yourself mightily mistaken and probably a bit embarrassed. And while you've thus been spared the inconvenience of returnable empties, *no* portion of *The Real Thing* ought to be eaten or drunk. This is a book, and recommended for external use only.

So just what have you gotten yourself into? What is a "real thing"? Well, Webster defines it as—let's see here . . . razorbilled auk . . . reactionary . . . realpolitik . . . but no "real thing" listed, not even the hint of a definition. Yet perhaps there lies a lesson: which *dictionary* is the real thing? Is it Webster? Which one of the many so called? Or the Oxford English, by virtue of its sheer bulk? And what about the heritage of Dr. Johnson's seminal work? Granted, he lacked an advisory panel—no Edwin Newman, no Tony Randall. Nonetheless, Johnson's dictionary deserves at least token consideration. We're in a quandary, and that never feels good.

You begin to understand now that the real thing isn't just the most popular, or the most famous, or the costliest, prettiest, oldest, biggest, longest, or anything else-est. It is, to use the powerful analytic tool rhetoricians call "tautology," the most *real* thing. It's a species' essential type. It's the one thing that most manifests the thing-hood of a given category of things, a quiddity. Got that? Good.

Sometimes the choices herein will coincide with the "bests" and "mosts" that lazier authors have depended on. But *The Real Thing*—and the far-from-capricious method of its creation—is vastly more complicated than any previous, superficially similar work.

The intent of the book is serious, but not solemn. Any idiot can assign the one-dimensional superlatives. It's not difficult to determine the "best." But today people demand more. In a world piling up with an ever-more-dizzying array of new things, informed citizens demand a professional's judgment of which are the *real* things. In other words, paraphrasing the French expert Peter Roget, you insist on knowing which are the authentic, quintessential, archetypal, genuine, actual, true, essential, pure, bona fide, heart-whole, blown-in-the-bottle, unalloyed, unadulterated, and singular things.

Of course we couldn't hope to pinpoint every real thing. Such an endeavor would overtax our resources and your attention span. Under no circumstances regard this book as you would a lover during your first dawn together, or the Civil Defense warden when he's explaining the inflatable asbestos tarpaulin; scrupulous attention is uncalled for. This is, rather, a preliminary how-to book that happens not to include instructions for flattening your tummy, collecting needlepoint shoulder holsters, or building a solar crockpot. Here you'll find nothing but the truth, we hope, yet something less than the whole truth. The entries are limited to life's compelling issues, the indisputably significant facts of existence like the "Tonight Show," aerial bombs, sainthood, and processed cheese snacks. You've seen children's paint-by-number sets: treat *The Real Thing* as a think-by-number kit for grownups.

Enough. Just flip to any page, and discover there a determinedly pithy chat about one or another real object, place, personage, institution, type, or aquatic mammal. That's all there is to it. Yet maybe a nagging question remains: How are you to know *for sure* if these judgments are trustworthy? You weren't born yesterday, but you're not unfamiliar with the dupe's role either. Relax: copies of my paperback companion volume—*Choicing: How to Decide Which "Real Thing" Book Is the Real Thing*—will be on sale soon at bookstores and supermarket checkout stands everywhere.

BEER

Budweiser is the real thing . . .
but Anheuser-Busch has it all wrong: Bud isn't the king of
beers, it's more like the citizen or infantryman of beers. This
is democracy! Our forefathers fought a war for freedom from
the yoke of Old World oppression, and every glowing Budweiser sign in every dark bar across the land is a welcome reminder to shun the aristocratic come-ons of precious brews
like Beck's, Watney's, Heineken, and St. Pauli Girl.

Beer is not anisette. You don't slouch around in some
comtesse's drawing room and sip Pabst from Waterford
snifters, saving the Courvoisier to chug after the Rangers'
game. Beer is for drinking, for throwing down your gullet as
though your innards hadn't been irrigated since July.

We pantywaists may like our occasional Heineken Dark,
but most of us are not tried or true beer drinkers. Who are
the guys and gals sucking up the vast oceans of foam the
American breweries spew out? They are your basic case-at-a-
sitting people: it's this elite underbelly that keeps the barley
malting and the hops effervescing, they who patriotically consume 80 per cent of the annual domestic production. This insatiable throng requires a constant infusion of beer as surely as
the rest of us need electricity, white sugar, thick hamburgers
and plenty of fresh air.

Not that they've got much choice of product. Today

there's just one beer company for every *forty* that existed before Prohibition, and five megabrewers sell more than two thirds of the 20 *billion* quarts we buy each year. A lot of numbers there, but numbers, as long as they stay in the realm of basic arithmetic, tend to go over big with beer drinkers. Get a few Buds down me and I can tell you like *that* how many inhabitants the city of St. Louis lost between 1970 and 1974 (39,000), or by how many lifetime home runs Harmon Killebrew bettered Mel Ott (62). Give me time to finish a six-pack and hell, I'll tell you Maravich's per-game scoring average at LSU (33 or 34, not including free throws). Numbers are good and blunt, handy pegs over which we can drape our minds while we toss back the Budweisers.

The competition? Miller Highlife ("The Champagne of Bottled Beer") gives champagne and the high life a bad name; Coors is Rocky Mountain Schlitz, and both should be repackaged and exported to Eastern Europe as engine coolant. Olympia is fair, but it's transformed fearfully little by its passage through the body; Pabst comes very close to Bud in temperament, but Blue Ribbon doesn't use huge Irish second bananas and huger draught-horses as television pitchmen. Anheuser-Busch knows what it's selling.

AFFECTATIONS

Feigning ignorance of one's native language, such as the Radcliffe graduate from Chicago's North Shore who stops herself mid-sentence, furrows her brow elaborately, and asks, "Oh, God, *what's* the word in English . . . ?"

is the real thing.

But there is an encyclopedia of also-rans, so many are the ways we get too big for our britches.

The phrase "have no" used instead of "don't speak"—as in "I have no Celtic"—is pretentious all right, but less horrifying than actually *speaking* Celtic.

A corollary outrage is the twit's frequent insistence that "it's absolutely *essential* to read Menander in the original Greek." The would-be pedant who announces that he's "read all of Goethe in the original Portuguese" won't win many stars, but at least we can laugh at his misfortune, as we do at the straggler's remark that he reads "Faulkner in the original English." (The line between the cretinous and the cryptic is thin.)

But affectation isn't limited to linguistic matters. Clam-digging, unless in service to a seafood restaurant, is a high-falutin exercise, and so are most of the pleasures overmonied urbanites manage to explore during New England summers. In the cities themselves, the sidewalks are rife with shanks of seldom-used squash rackets, each protruding rakishly from a handsome briefcase. But at least in this instance the racket's butt-end serves as a kind of low-tide warning buoy, a silent but unmistakable caution to steer clear. Commoner every month are expensive solar energy setups on the roofs of the gentry's homes, this decade's version of the garden party for Cesar Chavez.

Many are rankled by non-physicians who call themselves "Doctor." Dollars to doughnuts these poseurs were born in a Warsaw Pact country, or struggled through UCLA extension courses for seventeen years, or both. It wouldn't be a bad idea to make the use of the "Dr." title statutorily limited to men and women who've actually sliced flesh and dispensed drugs. (Those who might wriggle through the law's loophole—drug-dealing killers—would probably rarely take advantage of the opportunity. And you'd hear no objection from me even if knife-wielding druggies did demand to be called "Doc.")

There are plenty of pretensions we're unaccustomed to regarding as such. Being a beautiful, trilingual Eurasian is, when you come right down to it, a colossal affectation which we can condone no more than we do foreign cigarettes, expensive mustards, houses with names like Hillrise, collar pins, Oxford degrees, using the word "commonweal," having been in the OSS, graduates of American public schools who speak, with a tear, of their "third-form year," and people who profess a fondness for Matthew Arnold and watch nothing but public television.

The obsessive Anglophilism of PBS is typical of American affectation, which for some reason takes the form of pretending to be a boyishly middle-aged Londoner. This is George Plimpton's true vocation, frankly, and that of anyone else who pronounces "harass" correctly and "extraordinary" as if it had three syllables at most. Take Gore Vidal . . . *s'il vous plaît.*

UNPLEASANT SURPRISES

Forgive the redundancy.

Birth is a fairly compelling choice—you'll notice it's called the "birth *trauma*," and not the "birth frolic" nor even the "birth receiving line." In those first few postfetal seconds, if we have our wits about us, we make a solemn oath to avoid future surprises, most especially the ones which entail being manhandled under bright lights by a huge person wearing rubber gloves and a soiled green smock.

Shockingly, though, there are some who *relished* every ugly moment of their severance from umbilical paradise. There are those among us who found in their own, impatiently awaited births the chance to strive for the greatest, struggle to the top, to meet and conquer angst and antagonist alike. Ah, bloody birth at last! Let's grab for the brass ring and ford some mighty rivers! Let's hack through the wilderness and earn six-figure incomes before we're thirty! Let's get at this fray they call "life"!

(It is the Eskimos who tuck certain newborns into fast-moving ice floes and wave good-bye without a whimper or a regret.)

So we must search further, for the unquestionably universal, the invariably disconcerting. There is the first-grader's surprise at *gym class*, but the same babies who enjoyed obstetrics tend to become children well prepared for undressing with strangers in a stifling closet and climbing impossibly swaying ropes; universality nixed again. In roughly chronological order, then, there is: *the realization of one's mortality*: unpleasant without doubt, but the surprise with which we usually greet this bad news is a little false. Did we really believe that "Grandma went to a special happy place in the sky" as a reward for breaking her hip on the sidewalk? Just a bit later we learn that *lying isn't foolproof*—a surprise certainly, unpleasant to the extent that your parents were unpersuaded of the superiority of "reasoning" to a hard thwack across the butt. *Electric sockets* are a regular surprise package of unpleasantness. There's the dismay of *learning that astronauts are not smart*, and *vomiting for the first time*. There's *reaching the limits of cuteness*, when an unhappy-little-fella pout and smudged cheeks didn't seem to do the trick after a chemistry set crucible got out of hand and burned down the garage. (Similar but distinct is that wrenching discovery, much later, of *precocity*'s limits; it is the rare novel, for instance, praised by critics as "exceptional writing for a man of forty-one.") *Summer camp* is the classic case of a lonely hellishness touted beforehand as the best sort of old-fashioned fun. In sexual matters, *the sudden unavailability of women's breasts from late infancy through adolescence (at best)* is an unfathomable precursor of deprivation to come.

Which tugs us gawkily into *puberty*, the hands-down real thing of unpleasant surprises. For puberty isn't just a *single* horrifying surprise: no, as our various scars attest, it is a many-faceted circumstance that lingers on, for slow years. At irregular intervals, fresh bundles of new, weird hormones swim up and surprise the brain again, and just when you thought the last devastation was cleared up and all systems were stable, other bearers of bad neural news, equally unmerciful, goad the limbs and teeth and flesh into humiliating configurations. Puberty is designed to hit you where you live, which for the duration is that rubbed-raw, hungering larval libido. It's impossible to learn the ropes until it's too late. Bad acid filtered through dirty strychnine was never this awful. At eleven, you're looking forward to hot rods, french fries, geometry, and no bedtime; instead you're served up one deep and constant *faux pas.*

The worst is then past—one of life's few pleasant startlers—and the relative scarcity of surprises, pleasant or unpleasant, is adulthood's generous compensation for losing that overrated "sense of childlike awe." *Thomas Hardy* and *German films* are still to come, of course, and so is *responsibility, the loss of faith in science, no exchanges/no returns, pregnancy* (for some), and *finding out that love means a lot more than never having to say you're sorry.* And *work*—that is, the ultimate realization that you *must* do it—proves a real shocker for a few months. But from there on out it's all smooth sailing until your son comes home from college with a sequined Oscar Wilde T-shirt and a laser.

SUPERMARKETS

Safeway is the real thing . . .
even though shoppers who live east of the Mississippi or outside our nation's capital are unable to take part in the joys of
consuming, Safeway style. But every Westerner (and Wash-
ingtonian) knows well that Safeway supermarkets are the
purest expression of this purely American enterprise. No one
can resist the temptation to *buy* as they roll through a Safeway aisle, each big enough to accommodate a Panzer convoy.
If it weren't for the sprightly Muzak and arctic air condition-
ing, shoppers would stand and stare for hours at the fifty-yard-
long freezer case devoted to nothing but frozen fish sticks. A
seductive package here, there a glistening can, everywhere one
of Safeway's maddeningly infinite selection of merchandise.
Only the excitement of the checkout lines—the row of computerized Purchase Terminals stretches forever—keeps families from camping out, days on end, considering the mysteries
of Universal Product Codes, and free gifts for terriers and the
elderly. Being at Safeway is better than being at home.

And we needn't rely solely on our half century of domestic
experience to convince. Guess which American supermarket
chain has 448 outposts from Munich to Melbourne? Whose
savagely complete emporia are imposing shrink-wrapped gib-
lets and Potato Buds on every international cranny? Not
A & P, not Big Star, not Stop 'n' Shop, not Sloan's, not Pantry

Supreme, Giant, Alpha Beta, Richway, Hinky-Dinky, Food-town, Piggly Wiggly, Winn-Dixie, and certainly not Gris-tede's. Safeway, of course, is inlaying the bright stamp of American supermarketry all over the free world.

BREAKFAST CEREALS

Kellogg's Corn Flakes are the real thing . . .
because, come on, vitamin-fortified gypsumlike chips of corn
are what American breakfasts are all about. Our custom—
slurping cold cereal, the more innocuous the better—makes
for a clean placebo meal. Any other food so early in the day
might startle us.

But also in their favor, Kellogg's Corn Flakes were invented as a vegetarian treat for a ward of discontented sanitar-
ium patients. Whether or not we're taking a rest cure for
scrofula, we all need a quick and crunchy morning pick-me-
up, and I guess we ought to be mighty grateful to the
brothers Kellogg that we don't today drink laudanum with
our shirred eggs and cinnamon toast.

Before Battle Creek, Michigan, became synonymous with
K-E-double-L/O-double-Good, the town was something of
a Great Lakes Baden-Baden. Prosperous neurasthenics shuffled through the streets, not assistant brand managers or
box-top designers. By the turn of the century, the air was
heavy with the herbal steams and crank regimens of Victorian
sanitaria. Dr. John Kellogg operated the main spa in Battle
Creek, and with his brother Will, the detail man, Dr. Kellogg
set out to make a tasty health nugget from toasted wheat.
When wheat flakes worked, corn was not far off, and dis-
charged patients begged for more. In 1899 the pair formed

the Sanitas Nut Food Company and seven years later Will bought out brother John and began printing his own signature on every box of Toasted Corn Flakes. The Kellogg autograph has since evolved into today's stylized logo. But the personalized touch, Kellogg's Corp. says now, was Will's way of assuring customers that they were buying "the original . . . the real thing." That's good enough for me. As a blind, retired old codger during the Depression, William Kellogg would regularly have himself parked alongside the big Battle Creek plant because he positively loved to sit and listen to the roar and rumble of his corn-flaking machinery. A demure snap, crackle, and pop at home just didn't serve.

It's a surprise to learn that corn flakes are still the best-selling breakfast cereal on seven continents, like finding out that National Guard troops sing "Over There!" as they're airlifted in to quell a ghetto riot. I thought only people on the order of Buddy Ebsen and Dinah Shore ate corn flakes these days. I assumed that with short skirts and too much color TV had come the pre-eminence of Alpha-Bits or Cocoa Pebbles, Cap'n Crunch or Frankenberry. But no: box cars crammed with hot stacks of Kellogg's Corn Flakes are dispatched from forty-nine factories in twenty countries.

The only cereal man who gave Wm. Keith Kellogg a run for his money was C. W. Post. In 1892, when the Kelloggs were still content to humor consumptives and dowagers, Post bought a little farm on the outskirts of Battle Creek,* dead set on concocting a wholesome cereal *beverage*. (*Mm-mmm.*) Within a few years Post was selling runny white Postum, and the next year he ground out his first batch of Grape-Nuts, the morning meal for macho monks. If Grape-Nuts didn't remind the mouth quite so much of baked gravel, they'd have a good chance at edging out corn flakes. (In fact, Post came

---

* Mr. Graham, of cracker fame, was also a *fin de siècle* resident of Battle Creek and health-food fanatic. Battle Creek was to cereal what Paris, at the same moment, was to modern art. They get Cezanne, we get Sugar Smacks.

out with his own corn flakes simultaneously with the Kelloggs. Not being the savviest of modern marketers, however, Post called his cereal Elijah's Manna. It didn't sell, and Life is the closest thing to a religious cereal we have nowadays.)

In the course of learning more than I ever wanted to know about bran fiber and riboflavin content, I was granted a bonus by fate: the real thing in corporate public relations gibberish. The question: why is it that Kellogg's (and the rest) slathers sugar on all its cereals? "Sugar," their front office explains, "plays several important roles in the formulation of cereals."

> First, the sugar makes the cereal more palatable as it adds sweetness. Second, sugar contributes to the development of the golden brown color of the final product through the toasting process. Third, the addition of sugar to a cereal product during processing creates a distinctive product flavor, appearance and texture that cannot be achieved by simply adding sugar to the cereal at mealtime.

Ah-*ha*: they put in sugar because . . . it makes the cereal so good and *sugary*. That may make sense to consumers whose minds are already addled, abuzz with the fire of pounds of excess sweets, but it's pretty feeble dissembling for an outfit of Kellogg's size. Mobil manages to make me believe that great black oil spills are *good* for porpoises and seabirds.

FEARS

The fear of death is the real thing . . . and don't let anyone tell you different. People do, of course, constantly. "Death must be accepted as part of life's natural flow," we're instructed again and again by people who've never actually died themselves. "Death is not to be resisted or fought or feared." Yeah? Then what *is* supposed to scare us? Mexico? Losing the car keys? Pointy sticks?

Reasonable men and women will be scared out of their wits by a whole world of things. Like huge shopping centers and Christian snake-handlers and Hell's Angels. Those are all scary. Astrologers with goatees are scary. Nearly any animal is scary unless it's eating canned food from a little bowl or I'm eating it. Marsupials are scary regardless of the circumstance. Surely I'm not alone in my brooding fear that Rex Reed is the Antichrist, and that parthenogenesis will shortly emerge as America's most popular leisure-time activity. Dressing for success is scary. Other people's fathers are scary, as are state troopers, all-you-can-eat smorgasbords, a change in bowel or bladder habits, a sore that does not heal, obvious change in wart or mole, consulting your physician, Drāno, Italian headwaiters, calculus, small handguns, scorpions, Elisabeth Kübler-Ross, tumbleweed, marine life you can't see, Hammurabi's Code, and people wearing more than one leather garment. There are many, many things to fear besides fear itself.

But you'll note that nearly all of these bugbears are little more than the time-honored fear of death, thinly disguised. The fear of large, swarthy psychopaths carrying power tools, for example, is a common phobia. Death by any other name. If you try to persuade me that armed and menacing poor people ought to be accepted as part of nature's grand scheme, there'll be trouble. Even if the attacker has a No Nukes bumper sticker pasted on the side of his screaming twenty-one-inch chainsaw, even if bits of granola are stuck to the corners of his foam-flecked mouth, I will steadfastly refuse to welcome him as part of the Universe's eternal order. No Zen master I know ever had his imperturbability tested by a man gone berserk with dangerous Black & Deckers. Why do you think there are no lumberjacks in lamaseries?

If others wish to embrace death with a sage's equanimity, that's far out. I won't think less of people who use their own coffins as wine racks, or arrange for their ashes to be scattered over the co-op's herb patch.* Go with it. Beautiful. It's just that I see the natural flow of *my* life more along the lines of a rich, high-spirited wife, a rambling two-hundred-year-old house in the country, and a flock of smart and beautiful children who think they have the bestest dad in the whole wide world. Death can take a holiday as far as I'm concerned, and fly standby to boot.

* These are very likely the same folks who explore caves for fun. And in fact, it's spelunkers who risk the single scariest possibility there is. First, going into caves is unpleasantly frightful; the bats who call caves home are the animal kingdom's scariest creatures; bat droppings are, if not frightening, certainly unsettling; and lightning is second only to avalanches in Mother Nature's array of scary common phenomena. Anyway, spelunkers regularly run the danger of lightning striking deep within their caves, and detonating the mounds of bat guano collected on the cavern floor, thus causing a tremendous explosion. Among arcane fears, this must certainly be the real thing.

CARS

Listen: we both know that mass transit is a tidy way to ferry criminals and the elderly around our dying cities. But would you rely on a subway—even an express—to get you from Iowa City to Boulder in nine hours flat? Have you ever watched a double feature of *Teenage Goosebumps* and *Illiterate Tennessee Chain-Rapers* through the smeared windshield of a trolley car? Can you roll down your Metroliner window, turn up "Satisfaction" real loud and go cruising for fried foods? I-80 is there for a reason, or at least a pretext.

Any of the several hundred thousand extant 1964 *Ford Mustangs* is the real thing, but particularly light blue ones with rust just now creeping up over the fender edge. This was the original Mustang, and the first modernist American car. From zero to sixty in gas-squandering bliss, and no emission-control apparatus to make you feel like you're driving a low-tar cigarette or an ungainly chiropractic appliance. And when you whipped open the doors, no buzzer admonishing like some priggish foster parent. If you hankered to die senselessly in a smoldering snarl of sheet metal, that was your own business. The $2,368 sticker price freed you from further obligation.

In 1964, neither blitheness nor mawkish nostalgia nor toxic particulates were yet prohibited, and a car—just the car itself

—was still an occasion for giddiness. A mildly reckless lane change at dusk, or flooring it onto a Mass Pike entrance ramp in bare feet—remember, cars were once our pals, and Mustangs most of all. Riding the bus provides no vim.

DESSERTS

Dacquoise is the real thing . . .
because it elegantly performs the one true function of any
just dessert, which is to provide unseemly quantities of butter,
eggs, and sugar without attracting funny looks from parents
or guardians. Any real dessert must include these ingredients
and maybe a little chocolate, some nuts, and flour. (But the
flour's permissible only if its natural nutrients have been re-
moved, the hard brown kernels smashed and pummeled into
silky whiteness. If we really wanted whole-grain foods, we'd
strap on the nosebag and wander into a silo.)

These days it isn't easy to enjoy an authentic dessert, properly served. Settling down into a café seat for a midday
mound of sweet cholesterol is considered on a par with self-
mutilation. "You're *really* eating *that?*" asks the miscreant in
the down-filled bikini briefs as he jogs by, on his way to a dessert of dried lime rind and seawater. This is the sort of nutri-
tional zealot who'd have you eating groat pie, carob-and-celery
biscuits, or, worse, who serves fruit at the end of dinner and
pretends it's dessert. Fruit is not dessert. Fruit and expensive
runny cheeses are not dessert. They are pleasant-looking
foods, and may seem vaguely sophisticated, but always ask
yourself these three important questions when confronted by
a food posing as dessert:

1) Does it contain at least a pound of refined white sugar?

2) Is it somehow reminiscent of Versailles?

3) Do lower primates eat it in their natural habitats?

Yes, yes, no, and you may have yourself an acceptable confection.

A usually reliable test of a supposed dessert is to feed a smidgen to a child: kids don't make themselves sick on lemon *sorbet* in Perrier sauce, or desiccated figs.* It's alarming *ad hoc* recipes of Parkay and brown sugar and cream kids whip up on Saturday mornings before anyone's up, or on Saturday night with only the babysitter (herself a near-baby strung out on carbohydrates) conspiratorially on guard. Children don't sneak papaya-studded gelatin rings into their bedrooms for secret sessions of gluttony. No, they steal Mom's loose change to buy refrigerated cylinders of slice 'n' bake cookie dough and eat it, raw, in ten minutes flat.

A true dessert is just a studied, prettified version of these preposterous childhood concoctions. The dacquoise recalls all those innocent fantasies of sugary goo, three bowls full. A dacquoise is a dozen egg whites, more than two cups of powdered sugar, a whole *pound* of butter, some ground nuts, and no nutritive value—that's all that goes into the delicate cake with the fancy name. It takes hours to make and days to recover from a glistening chunk selfishly gobbled. We're talking hypoglycemic coma.

Controversy may well greet this choice. *Beignets fruits et fleurs* (deep-fried flowers and fruits) and *baisers de vierge* (sugared violets and whipped cream) each has its constituency. Those who prefer desserts with a fitting nonsense name (*zabaglione*, syllabub, shoofly pie) will find dacquoise

* The only reason to eat sherbet at all is to flaunt your polish by ordering exotic flavors like mango ice. The eating is an anticlimax to the ordering, however, a common disqualification for candidates in this category. Contrary to convention, *sorbets* don't do a very good job of "clearing the palate" between courses. Chewing a large ice cube or sipping from the finger bowls works better, and at the same time subtly indicates your contempt for the constraints of bourgeois etiquette.

pretentious, and connoisseurs of hothouse sculpture like *rêve de bébé* (pineapple, kirsch, maraschino, strawberries, and whipped cream) may think it insufficiently bizarre. Then there is that growing public which demands desserts with theatrical names: Glace Carmen; Bavarois Figaro; *charlottes opéra*; Soufflé Aïda; Coupe Emma Calvé; Fruits Sarah Bernhardt; Pêche Melba, the Bombes Falstaff, Othello, and Tosca; and, for those who will even eat a nondessert for dessert so long as it has an operatic namesake, Chicken *Tetrazzini*.

But the vogue for poultry desserts is really beside the point. Let's face it—the chore of plowing through six preliminary courses is a matter of keeping up appearances. We must admit that the whole of what we call a "meal" is simply an excuse to gorge ourselves on at least two helpings of some thick, sick, luxurious dessert, full of sugar and spice and everything unfashionably delicious, and then nibble on a few savories after.

Jack Daniel's is the real thing . . .
despite the fact that it's not technically a Bourbon whiskey.
But benighted nitpickers have no right telling us what's Bourbon and what isn't. Bourbon, some will whine in protest, is a
certain sort of corn liquor distilled in a 258.4-square-mile re-
gion of northern Kentucky. Jack Daniel's Old Time No. 7
Brand Quality Tennessee Sour Mash Whiskey dribbles into
being a bit south-southwest of the mandated wellspring of authentic Bourbon. Pay no mind to this misguided bunkum.
And don't let Jack Daniel's own marketing scheme, with its
premeditated folksiness, stir up hype-wary suspicions of fakery.
Those clever still-builders in Lynchburg know they've got a
good thing going; if they insist on pandering, let them. Their
product is sweet and hot and fine.

All Bourbonlike whiskey derives from a potent hodgepodge
of grains, a mash consisting by law of at least 51 per cent corn.
Ergo, the "corn-mash whiskey" of redneck legend. Two
things can ordinarily happen to used corn mash: it's fed to
pigs, or it's sold to another distiller, a distiller of *sour-mash*
whiskey like Jack Daniel's. And out of these great gallons of
sloppy seconds, together with some tempering virgin mash,
comes Old Time No. 7 Brand Quality Tennessee etc., etc. Ordinary Bourbon, then, is to Jack Daniel's as raw diamonds are
to the cut and faceted variety. (Both diamonds and Bourbon

start out as rotted plants, and both—together with the dog—are humankind's best friends.)

For me, Jack Daniel's was an uneasily acquired taste. Corn-mash whiskey, like Merle Haggard, rifles, the smell of alfalfa dehydration, and grimy carnivals thick with young blond sluts —all the very best of the American hinterlands—these were not properly fancied by children of midwestern parents like mine. But a little class-unconscious rebellion does the system good, I figure.

So be blunt about it. Do it right. Not just "Uh, Bourbon, please?" but a jigger of Jack Daniel's, neat, no ice or water. Better yet, no glass. Sip it—moderate to big sips—and let that rube essence dance down the esophagus.

Of course, Wild Turkey will do in a pinch (and Pinch will do in a Commonwealth nation), but only a flagon of Jack Daniel's will suffice for flagrant bawdiness. Revel in the vulgarity, now, and get *stupid*, you peckerwood.

LAW FIRMS

Davis, Polk & Wardwell is the real thing . . .
and though you may not give a hoot, you should. Leading lunatics of the vulgar left and right are in rare agreement here:
the affairs of the world are managed from the conference
rooms of a dozen big Wall Street law firms. You know—
Rockefellers and secret chartist cliques and the NSA and the
Trilateral Commission and Jews and Swiss-educated South
Americans—all the people who want to ship welfare mothers
to Boca Raton and fluoridate the Bermuda Triangle and sell
Tanzania to the Krupps—they've all connections to big Wall
Street law firms.

But even observers in reasonably good mental health admit
to the disproportionate clout of a couple hundred lawyers
clustered in lower Manhattan. You won't do well to ignore
them.

The real thing must be a gargantuan New York firm. More
to the point, it has to be an unimaginably stuffy Wall Street
firm. But this makes it tough. Because while our minds' eyes
see a panoramic sepia portrait of brilliant old legal clubbies,
that gentlemanly townhouse image is growing as unreal as the
house-calling country doctor with a heart as big as DeKalb
County. The New York barristers' polished power elite still
go through the motions, but that polish is wearing thin. The
cold steel core of money lust is showing through.

Davis, Polk & Wardwell occupies five floors of Chase Manhattan Plaza, all chrome and glass expanse barely softened by a good piece of art here and there. The clean hard offices are fogyish and Main Line in spite of these aesthetic odds. (For the old cartoon world of hand-carved Xerox machines and mahogany-paneled urinals, see Winthrop, Stimson and Etcetera, below.) The partners at Davis, Polk yet cling—maybe just a bit desperately—to their notion of civilized lawyering. The partnership roster could practically be a subsection of the Social Register. And that's a key: if a gentleman of the bar must sweat, he does it on the squash court or his boat, *not* practicing law.

A man named C. Payson Coleman more or less runs things. It's claimed that this is the man's christened name. But it sure sounds contrived to convey well-heeled sobriety, much as monikers like Tab Hunter and Charo are fashioned to reveal their bearers in a nutshell. Maybe the better law schools give their students new names before graduation, like Catholic teen-age confirmation names; I'm convinced "C. Payson Coleman" was specially designed to have "Esq." plugged on the end.*

The firm's other partner-of-note is one Lawrence Walsh. Remember the Paris Peace Talks? Mr. Walsh was one of the Nixonian envoys to those endless summits. He shined so in that capacity—successfully negotiating the shape of the conference table—that he skipped like a flat stone into the private sector as Davis, Polk's first-string litigator. (Which means Walsh is the partner who has to go to court and arrange bail for ITT Corporation, for instance, after it's been arrested and locked up in the special corporate cellblock at Riker's Island.)

Before Davis, Polk encamped in its current high-tech headquarters, the firm shuffled its briefs a short walk away at 15 Broad Street. A law firm called Cravath, Swaine & Moore—

---

* On the other hand, Charo would not be a good pseudonym for a young attorney eager to make progress in Davis, Polk's trusts and estates department.

in too many ways an outfit at the cutting edge of big-time law today—was a co-tenant at 15 Broad. And the story goes that from morning chit-chat in the elevator anyone could tell a Davis, Polk man from a Cravath guy: the Cravathers one-upped each other with tales of marathon work sessions and sly depositions. The fellows from Davis, Polk quietly discussed rock-climbing, or prospective luncheon entrees.

Not that there's any legacy of laid-back sensuality at Davis, Polk. The human beings Davis, Polk, and Wardwell are all dead, but John Davis was a blustery doer of important works from the very beginning. In 1924, only three years after he joined the firm, Davis was the Democratic candidate for President of the United States. Don't feel stupid: no one else remembers him either, except George McGovern, who takes solace from the fact that it was John Davis (and not McGovern) who suffered the greatest popular defeat in history. During the 1930s Davis screeched and howled what his partners and peers grumbled more discreetly, that F.D.R. and his goddam New Deal were opening up the goddam floodgates to communism. By 1953, when he was championing segregation before the Supreme Court, Davis had grown purely loony. But while you had Davis calling the Secretary of Labor a Red, you also had partner Allan Wardwell—"the Bolshevik of Wall Street"—flying Red Cross missions to Russia. Gentlemen are permitted their eccentric passions.

Cravath, Swaine & Moore is a hellhole. "Sweatshop" is the standard term for Cravath and firms like it, but long, long hours do not alone make Cravath a deadly place to practice law. Cravath, Swaine & Moore is a great shiny monster of a machine, pressing out functional pieces of work over, and over, and over again, with tool-and-die precision.

The firm sits above Davis, Polk physically, on the top floors of the Chase Plaza.* Cravath, Swaine & Moore has been itself

* It is Chase's tower, incidentally, in which a true "Rockefeller

since 1944. In his published history of the firm—available everywhere in paperback—Bob Swaine provides us Paul Cravath's Three Big Principles: 1) that his law firm be ruled by a single despot, 2) that lawyers be hired, fired, and promoted on merit alone (sons, clubmates, and classmates notwithstanding), and 3) that Cravath lawyers will do nothing but practice law, will have no outside business, no pet charity, and no yen for public service. Cravath's dream of a regiment of automatic superlawyers has come true.

Cravath's hundred-plus associates are baby-faced Fausts. Associates are the sweating, grindstone-embracing plebes who actually do the work for which CBS, Time-Life, and IBM dole out millions. And especially at Cravath, the associates are extraordinarily well paid. They all scramble for seven or eight years to reshape themselves in light of the ghastly Cravath ideal. They hope to be given very large sums of money every month for the rest of their lives.

The clear thrust is toward the Cravathization of the practice of law. Cybernetics, everywhere. A graying and a flattening. The creation of a new breed of legal technocrats who live comfortably, work hard, and die sad. There are bands of idiosyncratic holdouts, generally west of Westway and the Hudson.

But we mustn't plan on seeing many more William Nelson Cromwells, he of Sullivan and Cromwell. Long after the telephone was universal office equipment, Cromwell had no use for the blasted things, to the point of demanding that his lawyers communicate by hand-delivered notes or not at all. There was Colonel William Donovan (of the OSS and Donovan,

---

firm" resides. John D., Jr. was the godfather—some say the true parent —of his college chum Al Milbank's Milbank, Tweed, Hadley and McCloy. The only remarkable thing about Milbank, Tweed was the late Tweed: Harrison Tweed was a hard-living, thrice-married polo player who was wont to get naked and roam the beach fronting his house on Long Island. Dick Cavett owns the house now. He is never naked.

Leisure, Newton and Irvine), who began that firm's still extant tradition of mid-afternoon tea and cookies, all served from a cart trundled around to each lawyer's office. (It wasn't until 1974, when some Scrooge decided that an annual Pepperidge Farm bill of $40,000 was exorbitant, that the firm switched to wholesale purchases of Hydrox in bulk.) They say business is not great at Winthrop, Stimson, Putnam & Roberts, and that may owe to the old boys' reluctance to get in step with the new order, their unusual lack of the twitchy, craven mania to *produce*. Reasonable hours are still the rule at Winthrop, Stimson; going home at five-thirty is not a bad joke. Maybe it's true that Winthrop, Stimson and its gracious brothers are going to seed. Maybe it's true that calling cards, Episcopalian buff blue carpets, book-lined corridors, and wormy old scrivener's desks are frippery, at odds with fraction-of-an-hour billing and digital drudges.

But then it certainly *is* true that now, at last, non-whites and non-males and non-WASPs are plying justice in the chambers of the biggest and the best. So it doesn't make much sense to look Bakke, and sigh.

FAST-FOOD HAMBURGERS

Burger King's Whopper is the real thing . . .
even though at first, the home of the Golden Arches and
Countless Millions Sold seemed the natural choice. McDonald's Ray Kroc was, after all, the pioneer in the now saturated
field. And McDonald's has pulverized more cattle than many
countries have people, fried potatoes enough to feed Ireland
for a century, and gushed out soda pop sufficient to carbonate
Lake Erie (which might, incidentally, be an environmentally
sound idea). Compared to the $4 billion-a-year McDonald's
empire on which the sun (or at least the yellow neon) never
sets, every other burger vendor is a small fry.

But Burger King and McDonald's are equals on the franchise food basics: high-gloss interiors, high volume, and hy-
giene. Why does Burger King get the nod? How does this
copycat Pillsbury subsidiary beat out McDonald's, Burger
Chef, White Castle, A&W, Wendy's, and the born loser
named Dog 'n' Suds?

First because Burger King broils its die-cut patties on *con-
veyor belts*. None of this old-fashioned griddle bother. If it
worked for Henry Ford's Model A's, it can work for 2.7
ounces of lean (not to say anorectic) ground beef. Burger
King's Beef Systems Analysts have harnessed this linchpin of
American industrial might in a way that turn-of-the-century
mass-productionists would not have dared dream.

The Double Beef Cheese Whopper is the top of the line at Burger King, and what your order-taker calls, in an amplified screech, a *"D.C. Whopper!"* And it is excessively, grotesquely, pleasingly huge. Not a fat, vertical pile o' beef like Mom used to burn, but *wide* and *heavy* beyond all bounds of taste and good sense. The Whopper drips and droops and slides around in your childlike hands like some great organic discus.

Nor should we slight the "Have It Your Way" bounty of Burger King service. The pimply burger-meisters actually will mount your modular Whopper in any fashion you command: pickles, catsup, hold the onion and tomato; heavy lettuce, no, *more*; no pickles, extra mayo, hold the onion, extra cheese; extra onion, minus mustard, hint of pickle; hold everything but the lettuce and catsup, no, wait, pickles too, no, wait. . . . There are few values more plainly American than freedom of choice, and nothing more star-spangled than a confusing, entirely *unnecessary* freedom of choice.

NEWS MAGAZINES

Time is the real thing . . .
not simply because *Time* invented its genre. One way of looking at it is that *Time* is to *Newsweek* is to *U.S. News &
World Report*, as *Pravda* is to *Izvestia* is to the *Journal of the
Ukrainian Concrete Industries*. Or *Time* and *Newsweek* can
be considered as roughly equal Ivy League college news-
papers, with *U.S. News* the best high school paper in Ohio:
in any case it's six of one, a half dozen of the other, and a few,
at most, of the third.

After all, *Time* founded the modern style of newsmagazine
writing: journalism by committee, playing fast and Luce with
the truth, single paragraphs zigzagging between hard fact and
value-added factoid, with glib and appealing neologisms like
"Euro-terrorism" throughout. Innuendo lurks behind every
verb, interpretation pokes its way into the most cold-blooded
statistic. More than anything it's the uncanny ability of the
Time machine to give us, in Richard Rovere's words, prose "at
once trivial and portentous." (To *Time*'s credit, most daily
journalism can manage only one or the other, at best.)

Time has also been *the* forum, for all of us alive today, of
mainstream sobriety and the commonest kind of common
sense. The editors eschew extremism of any stripe as single-
mindedly as *Newsweek* craves modishness and *U.S. News* cul-
tivates bloodless conservatism. It's harder and harder to tell
the difference between the Big Two these days, but *Time*
remains the last, effervescent word in American newsweeklies.

INDUSTRIAL FOOD

Chee-tos are the real thing . . .
but on this I wouldn't stake my reputation. How do you
choose from a cornucopia brimming with Ho-Ho's, Ring-
Dings, barbecue-flavored fried pork rind, Pringle's "Potato
Chips," the Jiffy-Pop self-contained popcorn system, and
that classic funny food, Hostess Twinkies? (Twinkies, and
their Day-Glo pink relatives Snoballs are especially hard to ignore. As a lad I built a small cottage entirely from Hostess
Twinkies and Snoballs.)

Actually, the conventional term "junk food" may be unfair.
The various manufacturers prefer to call their products "convenience snack foods," according to a spokesman for the
American Junk Food Institute, a trade group. And we all
know there's nothing wrong with convenience. Great-
grandma may have had to treadle for hours at her rickety old
soya-paste extruder, and it took gramps three days' ride to
fetch the diglycerides and vegetable stabilizers. Whole pioneer communities would share a single box of Pop Tarts for
years. But those were inconvenient times.

Arrayed on the shelves of today's convenience grocery store
are tempting heaps of convenience snack foods, all available
for purchase twenty-four hours a day. Grab an overstuffed bag
of Chee-tos (the regular kind or the new, crunchy style) and
tear that cellophane asunder. Take a hearty lungful of unmis-

takable Chee-to bouquet: *mmmmmmmm!* Forget that they look exactly like the squiggly Styrofoam descendants of excelsior. Don't be alarmed by the Chee-tos' radium orange color: it's supposed to symbolize the color of cheese, not *be* it.

With some practice anyone can learn to appreciate the Chee-to appeal. It's true that nothing in nature shares the color, smell, texture, or taste of Chee-tos. But it's time we transcended our outmoded notion of "the four food kingdoms." Chee-tos, we know now, are part of the long neglected *fifth* food group. It's probably all right to down your daily quart of milk and ample portions of meat, grains, and leafy vegetables. But if you or your children are passing up the Chee-tos and Fresca, you could be depriving yourselves of important carcinogens.

Unlike most inconvenient foods, Chee-tos aren't "chewed." Disintegration may be the closest word in any Indo-European language to describe what happens to Chee-tos in the mouth. And don't expect a burst of hearty Cheddar flavor, for again, what you experience is an artful *representation* of cheese's taste.* What's wrong with that? The ability to use symbols is what distinguishes man from the lower species. You don't see dolphins snacking on Jeno's Pizza Rolls, do you?

A brunch of tofu and peach nectar may be all the rage today, or tomorrow. But Chee-tos, the Connie Stevens of foods, endures.

* Other artists working in the junk-food medium have interpreted "cheese taste" differently. The tiny crackers called "Cheez-It" tend toward a more oily robustness in their rather too intense evocation of the Cheddar ideal. And while the derivative "Cheese Nips" are formally similar, they are less stridently cheesy than "Cheez-It." The more recent "Cheese Kisses" reject realism altogether: you're never sure whether to eat them or rub them on blisters, and the taste and texture are reminiscent of not-quite-rancid soybean curd. The pop novelty of junk cheeses—the aerosol cheeses of the late 1960s—seems less amusing as the years pass.

BORING AMERICAN CITIES

Salt Lake City, Utah, is the real thing . . .
even given the particularly stiff competition from boring
burgs such as Bakersfield, California; Hartford, Connecticut; Columbus, Ohio; and that sandtrap-of-the-Southwest,
Phoenix, Arizona. Indeed, we suffer an embarrassment of
riches when it comes to tedious towns and cities. From Balti-
more, the city that wishes it didn't exist, to the gray monot-
onies of Providence (where Divine invocation has turned
into the continent's place-name joke), the country teems with
urban black holes that make Philadelphia seem like the
Athens of the Delaware Valley.

But back to Salt Lake City. Its very name is a dim flicker
("Hey, let's build a city by this here salty lake!"). But that
founding witlessness can be forgiven when it's remembered
that after two decades of legal harassment, killing winters,
marauding Native Americans, and desert heat, cleverness was
the last thing on the Mormons' 1847 agenda. Fatigue and
world-weariness are no sins; being a Mormon, however, is
harder to excuse.

What kind of city could be expected from a colony of
suicidally stoic bigamists, a people who don't drink liquor
(not even cordials), coffee, or tea, who consider checkers a sin,
and whose faith derives from some sixteen-hundred-year-old
South American gold tablets given by an angel called Moroni

to a prophet named Joe Smith in upstate New York? It's a pity that after the Mormon Conquest of Utah, this religious wackiness never vivified Salt Lake city life.

The city—whose population of 200,000 falls neatly into that too-big-for-quaintness-but-too-small-for-excitement range —sits appropriately in a vast, arid valley between undistinguished mountain ranges. The effect upon approach is that of a bleached color snapshot taken on that 1959 vacation trip nobody much remembers.

It can be hard to understand how Salt Lake City remains oppressive, given its nearly great symphony orchestra and feisty ballet ensemble. Maybe it's the town's industries: one of the nation's most obscure military installations—Hill Air Force Base—is close by, and employs a hefty proportion of Salt Lakers; weapons manufacture pays the rent for many; and copper, that most melancholy metal (why do you think it turns green?), is Salt Lake's economic backbone. Perhaps the clouds of dangerous gases that pour out of Kennecott's smelters account for the city's unspeakable torpor.

The Lord said that the meek shall inherit the earth. In this God-forsaken part of it, the prophecy is unmercifully manifest. Salt Lake City, Utah, is the largest city in the home state of the Osmond family, the place where you need a permit to buy a cocktail (and then only on alternate Tuesdays between Lent and Ramadan), the city Gertrude Stein was *really* talking about when she said "there's no *there* there," an aluminum-sided monument to the fanatical, four-wheel-drive Babbitry of the New West. If Nebraska is "where the West begins," Salt Lake City is where it begins to pall.

On the other hand, there are a lot of ski resorts nearby, in addition to Robert Redford.

BROTHELS

Rebecca's, in Acapulco, Mexico, is the real thing . . .
because it's neither as dreamy as the plush sexual salons of
Paris nor as adventurously unhygienic as the grubby fuck-huts
in Tangier's Old Quarter. A sensible whore-monger naturally
wants a little of both in his flesh-market dalliances. What's
the fun in sexual exploitation if it isn't a little bit the powdered master and his pliant young chambermaid? And yet, at
the other extreme, who can relax fearing the inopportune appearance of some crazed cousin Mustafa, scimitar flailing?

Acapulco is a dandy place for a whorehouse. The town was
genuinely chic for only an instant, years ago, and has slipped
toward tacky disrepute ever since. It is Reno-on-the-Sea, run
by Mexicans and without gambling, a made-for-TV tropical
resort. The beaches elsewhere are more unspoiled and picturesque, and better surfs (if not more deadly ones) exist up and
down the Pacific coast. Acapulco still plies its reputation for
exotic glamour through weary and wearying promotion of
the supremely and very much famous Cliff Divers who risk
lifes-and-limbs nightly, two shows ¡(eight and eleven-thirty)!

Rebecca's is set way up on a jungly mountainside, one of
the Sierra Madre del Sur which surround Acapulco Bay. Anyone in town can tell you how to get there, but only the bell
captain at your expensive MAP hotel will. He'll even have his
little brother chauffeur you there after the requisite exchange

of pesos and virile grins. The road is dark, steep, winding and paved barely. Many sense imminent shakedown or injury during their initial passage into these unknown parts. Others are too sodden or confident in their Yankee invulnerability to notice. Neither is quite right: an expectant ambivalence is the correct emotion to feel as you come to a stop at the frumpy complex of patios and gazebos at 10 Cuidado Road.

When you show up at Rebecca's on a slow night in a fast American car, you are made to feel pleasantly like a friend of Frank Sinatra's newly arrived in Vegas. The clutch of pulled-together hostesses—whose strange synthetic get-ups at last give meaning to "scantily clad"—mob the visitors, all giggly and solicitous. They're really very nice, as is Rebecca's itself. Not one of those horribly clean white sex factories endemic to Scandinavia, but neither does it seem that the place is owned and managed by a consortium of germs. It's comfortably seedy: the stucco is cracked, and cute reptiles dart among pieces of rattan furniture spread out over the main plaza.

What putatively happens in white efficiencies and sweltering cabañas all over the world is pretty much what goes on at Rebecca's. Nobody comes here to fulfill nurse/pillory/chocolate sauce fantasies, and the mirrored *mise-en-scènes* of *Le Balcon* get played out elsewhere, if at all. This is pretty gritty luxury, but the experience is as it should be: prosaic, and marginally pleasurable. *Viva.*

FUN THAT ISN'T

All large discothèques, and especially those modeled spiritually on Studio 54, in New York, are the real thing. I'm not forgetting zoos or square dancing or college reunions, the sports pages, Halloween, beach antics, performances of Brecht, or archery, each of which figures prominently in this realm. Others will scream that I've slighted caramel apples, esoteric forms of poker, tequila, impulsive military enlistments, circuses, and handicraft instruction. Each a righteous claimant. But the astute among you have already figured that all unpleasant fun—by my reckoning, anyway—is either noisy, smelly, or difficult. It is indeed, and discothèques at their truest are nonpareil on all three counts.

Not so long ago, "discothèque"—like "mall" and "marriage"—meant something quite different. But gone for good is the trippy innocence of Whiskey à Go-Go and its kind. After Lyndon Johnson died it was Studio 54 that sucked in Mica and Rod and Roy and Vitas and Tatum and C.Z. and *every* carefree, mad young deviate. Nowhere else was the contest for status played out nightly in such harsh and wanton fashion—save perhaps at some particularly savage initiation rite in the thickets of tribal Malawi. Midnight after midnight they still stand outside amid chuckholes and grit, the immobilized throngs beckoning, begging, bleating to be pulled inside. You get the feeling no one here would clap to keep Tinker Bell alive unless she had a good press agent. "Steve . . . Steve . . . *please,* Steve?" they would mew (and will again), each itchy to catch the evasive eye of the little owner. Most nights it was this same felonious monk "Steve" who—alone—seemed to be having a measure of real fun. And gosh: who wouldn't get a heady rush in the exercise of the face-to-face power he wielded exclusively and capriciously? An executive vice-president is permitted the occasional thrill of having a willing protégé by the short hairs, of sneering "*Sue* us, bub!" at some impotent victim of his clout. But what gray-flanneled man gets to yea-or-nay—in a blast of blissfully *public* barks—the existential worth of several hundred extravagantly dressed adults? Do you dole out petty favors to your betters, and get thanked with an obsequious ooze that might have embarrassed a suzerain during fief-granting season? In the overnight ascension and exile of Studio 54's runty, lumpenprole emperor—in that dizzy swirl you have the beginnings of an angle on this whole slicked-back, unkind business. Now, at least, Studio 54 has turned literally decadent.

For all their megawatts of electronic gimcracks, Studio 54 and Xenon and Bond's and the rest are cold, cold hangars. Freeze-dried profligacy. Imagine your high school prom squad the beneficiaries of a sum in the low seven figures, and the prom theme not *Rose in Bloom,* or *Camelot,* but a gracelessly rendered Classics Illustrated *Decameron.* And imagine all of that, if you can bear it, screwed into a metallic future where a junta of swinging headwaiters runs the world, where prudence of any kind is frowned upon. It can all be that disheartening.

A few words concerning the ostensible *raison d'être* of serious discothèques: dancing, that is. Sure, some of the voluptuaries shake it up on the dance floor. They shimmy, straight-faced, washed in neon or flash-frozen by the murderous strobes. But no Tony Molineros swagger in and mesmerize this fierce clientele, for dancing doesn't matter. You're not at all likely to see Diana Vreeland doing a latter-day Watusi with limber boys from Queens in Qiana. No, these discothèques are places for dancing like my mother's Sewing Club was an organization devoted to thimbles and pinking shears. They called it their Sewing Club, and even managed an occasional stitch or two, but the point was a fancy lunch, clucking conversation, and low-grade gossip. In other words a front, just like the discothèque of the moment—except that Mom and her friends did not wear gold lamé jumpsuits, bare their bosoms, and sniff cocaine in the bathroom. Not that I ever saw, anyhow.

COLAS

Coke really *is* the real thing . . .
darn it, and there's no cute way to avoid saying so.

A case can be made for Pepsi, even though it lacks an
urban monument to itself: Atlanta is a wholly owned leisure
service of Coca-Cola, whereas Pepsico is just one more right-
wing food combine. But Pepsi does have more calories than
Coke—ten more carmelized empties per twelve-ounce bottle—
and since maximizing sweet-heat units is the natural reason
for drinking pop, Pepsi wins on points. But not on essences.

Down below the 35th parallel, where the folks suck up
brown soda ferociously, little credence is given to this slick
"Pepsi Generation" hogwash. Oh, you might find a heretic
here and there who drinks RC on the sly, but Southerners
never stop pausing for the pause that refreshes.

(And unabated Coke consumption doesn't peter out at the
Rio Grande. Mexico and the rest of Latin America are awash
in the stuff, Coke in zip-top cans being as highly prized as
Gucci doodads in the States. Like their Indian ancestors of
decades past, modern Hispanics make good use of every part
of their prey. Granted that Coke is no bison, one still marvels
at this waste-not-want-more ingenuity: broken shards of Coke
bottles are cemented to the tops of garden walls as a decora-
tive menace, the caps are used as currency throughout much of
Paraguay, and whole families call empty wooden Coke cases
home. It's a bright day in many a Peruvian child's life when
he moves into his very own six-pack.)

COUNTRY CLUBS

The Country Club in Brookline, Massachusetts,
is the real thing . . .

or, if you please, the definite article. This is not the coy neighborhood nickname for the Brookline Country Club. It is, simply, *The Country Club.** If you've always been confused
about the meaning of *sui generis,* you may now unmuddle.

Like so many real things, the country club is as peculiar as
it is peculiarly American. Yet what's queer here is that these
obsessively manicured pseudo-manors are antithetical to everything we're supposed to hold dear, nay, to the American
Way itself. (There, I've said it. And as long as I've gone this
far I'll admit I've always wondered why Joe McCarthy wasted
his time on debating-society Reds instead of harassing the
true subverters of our nation's legacy, those two million citizens who might reply with an unflinching, uncontrite "yes" if
asked: "Are you now, or have you ever been, at a party where
golf tees were used as swizzle sticks?")

"*Un-American?*" you cry. "Smarty-pants bushwah!" Not so
fast, Jack. Name another American institution so widely em-
braced yet so unabashedly antidemocratic. There is a straight

* I do apologize to the members for causing the name of their es-
tablishment to be printed (twice, no less) in italics. I know you disap-
prove of jazzy typography, but I did refrain (as I promised) from
using boldface or red ink.

line from Jefferson and Tocqueville to drive-in theaters and land-grant universities. Country clubs are a mutant strain.

Most country clubs are the petty bourgeoisie putting on airs. They're the savings-and-loan vice-president strutting about in double-knit jodhpurs. They're the pathologist's daughter Suzi driving her brand new 'Vette into a water hazard after one too many Margaritas. The country club is a tipsy Phyllis Schlafly getting goosed by a randy Gerald Ford, it's Ed McMahon showing off his gallstone keychain to Elliot Richardson during the every-other-Tuesday-night Luau Smorgasbord, it's Erma Bombeck talking cellulite with Maureen Dean, and Bert Convy's wife comparing mortage payments with some Lyndon Johnson daughter.

But "country club" is a broad and inexact term. A good 98 per cent of America's four thousand-odd country clubs have the feel of nothing classier than a nonstop Kiwanis Barbecue-and-Vegas Night. Omaha's Field Club, for example, and Easthampton's Maidstone are both country clubs in the same way that your baton-twirling niece and John Gielgud are both entertainers. Still, one in twenty-five American bread-winners happily ponies up a grand or two every year for the privilege of country-clubbing it. But few among that horde would be permitted within chipping distance of The Country Club's primrose sancta.

The Country Club opened in 1882, its grassy acreage a short morning's carriage ride from the townhouses of Beacon Hill and Back Bay. Peabodys, Shaws, Adamses, and Ameses were the founders of this Brahminic playpen. It is Peabodys, Shaws, Adamses and Ameses—together with nine hundred cousins, cousins' cousins and a smattering of clubbable friends—who today shoot and putt and curl on the Club's calming grounds. Unlike the great majority of American country clubs, membership here requires more than merely having skin, belt, and shoes in matching white. The club buildings are comfortably rickety, by some Puritan magic kept in a perpetual state of tasteful disrepair. The staff is mostly (or at least most prominently) central-casting Irish: short, wiry, red-faced men who seem honored to iron your newspaper and freshen your Scotch rocks. No A-frame clubhouse here, no Interstate Highway unction.

Exclusivity, of course, is the thing. Of that oft-mishandled Old World quality The Country Club reeks. These gentlefolk, rich and less-than-rich, really are different from you and me. Even the caddies are high Episcopalian, and the horses have substantial trust funds. Thousands of clubs and associations have the temerity to exclude blacks and women and other undesirables from membership, but few others can articulately justify what they're doing, and believe it themselves. For these ultimate Yankees, "elitist" isn't a pejorative.

Every country club is a public celebration of inequality. That may be abhorrent. But The Country Club succeeds in being abhorrent attractively and that, I suppose, is not without value.

SCOTCH WHISKY

The Glenlivet is the real thing . . .
for reasons exactly opposite those justifying Jack Daniel's designation in BOURBON (see pp. 20–21).

Drinking Glenlivet makes you feel as though you're Antony Armstrong-Jones, up at the Viscount Runnymede's shooting lodge for a long weekend of bloodsports. If you wear tweeds or touch a Purdey shotgun while sipping Glenlivet, you might actually become Snowdon, and suddenly start divorcing princesses and snapping wry black-and-white portraits of celebrities. Use your own good judgment: it may be inconvenient for you to metamorphose into a British nobleman-by-marriage during lunch, for instance. If nothing else, the waiter will almost certainly expect a larger tip.

There's one last important difference between the real things of Bourbon and scotch. Jack Daniel's is coincidentally the best *and* the real example of its kind, whereas Glenlivet is merely quintessential. The best scotch, if you care, is Laphroig, a near-syrup the color of strong tea. Laphroig is a kind of distant, privileged cousin of Bourbon's, and each is a bit embarrassed by the other's existence, although they still exchange Christmas cards.

BASKETBALL PLAYERS

Dr. J is the real thing . . .
and among the clearest choices in the book. There's no contest. Julius Erving is called "Dr." because some playground teammate said "he knows how to operate" and he "makes you feel good." Dr. J *does* make you feel *real* good when he gallops down the court, zags under the basket and springs straight up into the air for a slam dunk in and through. Even from the top of the bleachers it's like an elbow in the solar plexus—literally breathtaking, that is—when the Doctor cuts out for the fast break, and with the ball in one expansive hand lifts off three yards from the basket and ka-*choong*. Julius Erving makes splendidly tuned defensive men feel like a bunch of spazes. Only if cheetahs had hands could the sport be better, and some young jungle cat might not be able to pass through the NBA Hardship Rule.

Bob "Big Mac" McAdoo can indeed do, but he's too tough. (McAdoo likes to scream *"In your face!"* at his guards right after a shot.) Lloyd Free, "The Prince of Mid-Air," is too much the fast-talking jive artist, hubris in motion. Connie "The Hawk" Hawkins was the first of the fully space age players, and he was fabulous, but he got screwed by smoothies and bagmen. George "The Ice Man" Gervin (his son's called "The Cube") doesn't look right, his body so like a mechanical pencil. Earl "The Pearl" Monroe—who's second only to fur-coated Walt "Clyde" Frazier in sartorial snazz—is sort of a reggae player: his jerky, idiosyncratic style makes every shot an off-rhythm surprise. U.S. Senators (such as, for instance, say, oh, Bill Bradley) are disqualified from contention. Ball-hogging "Pistol Pete" Maravich, Kareem Abdul-Jabbar, and Oscar "The Big O" Robinson lack Dr. J's absolute power to stun. (Besides which Mr. Abdul-Jabbar has no nickname. Basketball has spawned more pet names than any ten second-grade classes. That's misleading, actually, since most players' nicknames are self-appointed, requiring a good deal more chutzpah than the run of seven-year-olds possess. "Super" John Williamson told an interviewer that the "players around the league call me 'Super John' because I'm so good." The guy asked Williamson if he didn't "think maybe they call you that because that's what you call yourself?" "That could be, too," he conceded.)

Dr. J's wife is named Turquoise, and they've named their children Cheo, Jazmin, and Julius III. Dad wears size 15 sneakers, and was sold to the 76ers for $3 million. It was a sound investment. Philadelphia has a lot more going for it in goose-pimpling Dr. J than in ten thousand cheese-steaks and Liberty Bells.

Doc Watson is the real thing . . .
and thus not much fun to talk about. Born blind fifty-some
years ago in Deep Gap, North Carolina, Watson is a rustic
dream of pure folksiness. Started picking banjo with stubby
six-year-old fingers, taught himself to play schoolboy harp,
and bought his first guitar from Sears, Roebuck. Doc's first
public performance was at The Old Time Fiddlers' Convention up the road to Boone, and he made his reputation playing tunes at Baptist socials and boondock radio stations.
He's still playing and singing, and earning a living as a fave
rave of the folk *cognoscenti* who've had the lifelong disad-
vantage of not living in tarpaper shanties. But we mustn't
judge Doc Watson by the company who keeps him. He is
great. His music is low-key romp, one good man's variant on
a gnarled musical root. He's as real as they come, Eugene
Gant's handicapped little brother who liked it just fine down
home and never saw much use in writing new words. Doc
Watson is perfect, but no fun.

Pete Seeger is fun. It's fun to learn that his father was a
Harvard-educated professor of ethno-musicology, and that
primitive Pete himself was a New York preppy and Harvard
man. It's amusing to ponder that Seeger was only the first to
ride Woody Guthrie's mythic coat-tails, a folkie *modus
operandi* later refined by Bob Dylan with his presumptuous

pilgrimage to Guthrie's deathbed. And it's kind of a cheap thrill to witness the transformation of a Carnegie Hall commie into Cap'n Pete, ecology nut.

But there are still more kicks to be had from a peek at the contemporary female folk singers. Mimi Farina was enough to make you forswear petting with girls who understood metrical feet. The McGarrigle Sisters—wallflowery hippie wraiths with the luck of an apposite Scotch-Irish surname— are more than passable singers when they don't attempt French. Their literal sisterhood puts them in contention here: the synchrony of this underfed pair is vaguely spooky, and apropos. As the daughter of a nuclear physicist, Joan Baez may live any way she chooses, but one wonders just how all her acts are "part of the larger context of attempting to prevent murder." There hasn't been a murder at I. Magnin for years, and Bloomingdale's has pretty much discontinued its policies of genocide.

Joni Mitchell is more fun than a barrel of Sarah Lawrence freshpersons, even though she now seems determined to transmogrify into a jazz interpreter. Joni, unlike Guthrie (jailed), Seeger (blacklisted), and Baez (jailed and disliked), never suffered under the heavy thumb of death-culture reaction. Roberta Joan Anderson Mitchell, now nearing forty, was never obliged to scratch her lyrics on the wall of a prison cell with a piece of charred paraffin.*

Everybody knew a girl like Joni. As a pale and precocious child in Alberta, Canada, she "used to keep pressed flowers in a scrapbook . . . (and) scribbled poems on the backs of notebooks when I got bored." Oh, yes. Joni has been scribbling poems ever since, but what a refreshing sense of humor the once-brooding gal has developed. "I feel like I'm married to this guy Art. I'm responsible to my Art above all else."

---

* Unless you consider it a life sentence in solitary confinement to be a woman artist struggling to express herself openly and honestly within the straitjacket of Western patriarchal society. Many technically sane people do.

Joni has plowed through the pop-music pantheon in her search for a soulmate as self-absorbed as she. You'd have thought that in Leonard Cohen and James Taylor she'd find just the stereo confessional she sought. But maybe Leonard and James and the rest razzed her for her insistence that a Persian rug and a vase of roses accompany her onstage. Or maybe there is an actual human being, Art, back in Canada, to whom Joni's sleeve-mounted heart belongs.

Joni thoughtfully prints her lyrics on every album, a custom happily falling into disuse among less cheeky singers. "I hang laundry on the line when I write," she explains. But she finds that as a result, critics "make judgments and it's none of their business. It almost makes me decide not to write anything but fiction, but I have to do my own thing." Let us pray that we shall never be forced to choose between listening to a Joni Mitchell record and reading a Joni Mitchell novel. But for now, let's get back to doing our own thing: making judgments that are none of our business.

I'll take the punks' unearned cynicism over Mitchell's sappy synesthesia any day. And the real sadness is that Joni's voice is a wondrous instrument, rare and otherworldly. But since singer-songwriter is thought in too many quarters to be an indivisible hyphenate, Joni is indulged her poetic airs.

But that doesn't discourage sensitive, college-educated young women with two or more cats from buying and worshiping Joni's deadpan Zeitgeist. And these fans—frizzy-haired, herb-tea-swilling children's book illustrators all—know every word of every song. And as if the record-jacket transcriptions weren't enough, *they play the records.* There is in fact an unwritten oath among true lovers of Joni that one of The Records must be played, loudly and on an inadequate record player, every morning before nine, earlier and louder when rain is forecast. Especially on Saturday mornings, after a night of mean-spirited sex due to existential vapors, or too much Cinzano, or some bittersweet something.

BEAUTY QUEENS

Lynda Lee Mead, the 1960 Miss America
is the real thing . . .
because she was twenty years old, from Natchez, Mississippi,
and it was 1960. Also, her answer to the obligatory current-
events question as I recall it—"Lynda Lee, do you want peace
on earth or not?"—was learned and provocative. (One report
has the thirty-nine-year-old Ms. Mead as the assistant chief of
the CIA's Darky Affairs Desk.)

"Musical comedy" is the synonym here: a featherbrained crossbreed of folk dancing and light opera with casts the size of small towns and plots as flimsy as tracing paper. A good musical comedy is a big, fresh, million-dollar cheesecake, glazed with some cheery domestic moralism and served up with the rote bonhomie of a skilled call girl.

Nothing like *Elvis the Legend Lives*, for instance. Elvis impersonators are great in Route 66 roadhouses belting out a flat "Hound Dog" over jerryrigged jukebox loudspeakers. But for Broadway, such entertainments are like most Stephen Sondheim productions: deadly self-serious and more intriguing on paper than on stage.

A true Broadway show needn't be ignorant of highest culture. Take, for example, the sketch in *Two's Company* (1952) about a man who bought a Frank Lloyd Wright house that blended so perfectly with its environment he'd never been able to find it. We seldom get whimsies like that anymore, nor songs like "Lottie of the Literati" (*New Faces of 1936*) that griped, "*No matter who said it, Dorothy Parker gets credit.*" And the American musical's reputation for silly piety isn't altogether earned: for *Strike Up the Band* (a dumb joy-thumper of a name if there ever was one), Ira Gershwin wrote the lyric: "*We're in a bigger better war/ For your patri-*

otic pastime./ We don't know what we're fighting for—/ But we didn't know the last time."

And the lyric is the thing. On Broadway they've sung of everything from broccoli ("You're the Top") to Hershey bars ("They All Laughed"), and from "April in Paris" (*Walk a Little Faster*) to—truly—"April in Harrisburg" (*All in Fun*, 1941 [the same year Enrico Fermi became seriously enamored of small nuclear explosions]).

Because Broadway musicals are designed unashamedly as entertainments, mass appeal is as important to the equation ("let X equal *profits* . . .") as tunes-you-leave-the-theater-humming. Most egregiously conceived to please more of the people most of the time, there was one show called *Kosher Kitty Kelly*, and another that ran as *Toplitzky of Notre Dame*. (And in fact, the choreographer Jerome Robbins, apparently unmindful of the ancestry of the roving punks at his New York doorstep, originally intended *West Side Story* to be the tale of a pair of ill-fated *Irish* and *Jewish* lovers. Perhaps this conception was redrafted out of town, what with tryout audiences unmoved by the spectacle of Jewish gang members litigating the Irish toughs into submission, nor by the lyric, "*Naomi! I'll never stop saying Naomi!*") In another, still stranger transposition of cultures, Al Jolson appeared as "Monsieur Al" in a show called *The Wonder Bar*, and sang, in full natural whiteface, a song called "Ma Mère."

But not propriety, taste, or even good sense have served to bridle the novel imaginations of Broadway showmen. There was the 1926 show *Betsy*, in which an orchestra consisting entirely of harmonicas played "Rhapsody in Blue," and *Scandals of 1924*, with a number in which dozens of chorines formed parts of a giant handbag.

Enough of this soft-shoe badinage, you say. Get to the point. *Anything Goes* (1934) is the real thing. The show began life as a libretto, on which P. G. Wodehouse collaborated, about a balmy group of shipwrecked passengers. (See under SITUATION COMEDIES, pp. 59–62, "Gilligan's Island.")

The sets were built and the show was in rehearsal when a cruise ship burned and sank off New Jersey, killing 125. Revision was indicated. Howard Lindsay, the director, asked Russell Crouse to work with him (for the first time) on a new book—one which had to incorporate the existing scenery, songs, and cast, and sidestep recent tragedy besides. The tunes were Cole Porter's, among them "You're the Top" and "I Get A Kick Out of You." Ethel Merman starred as Reno Sweeney, evangelist-turned-chanteuse. Tap-dancing on the poop deck, singing from portholes, lines and lyric chockablock with spanking-smart vivacity; who could ask for anything more?

NEW ENGLAND TOWNS

Deerfield, Massachusetts, is the real thing in this category, beating out stiff competition from Kent, Connecticut, and Damariscotta, Maine. In Deerfield, it is *always* dawn or sunset, making for a picturesque, light-dappled vista anywhere you look, at any time. The main street of the town is quaint but not kitschy. Sure, there are plenty of restored colonial storefronts and a few too many salty old shopkeepers, but Deerfield has mercifully kept down the Ye Olde Plumbing Supplies Shoppes that disqualify so many other contenders. There are the requisite number of uninteresting historical monuments dotting Deerfield, but nothing like the patriotic nostalgia that overwhelms Concord, Massachusetts. You may not have the ivy-covered women's college out of which hordes of long-legged patrician beauties stroll, but you have got Deerfield Academy, one of those second-tier New England boarding schools that seem to admit its boys as much on the basis of their spotless complexions as on academic grounds. Then there's the graveyard where those deceased after the eighteenth century are considered *arrivistes,* and the charmingly unplanned country lanes, whose cobblestone tributaries wander between rude stone fences and fine old barns, past a perfect tableau of meadows, hills, ponds, and thickets. Deerfield, friends, is the real thing.

NAMES

George Miller is the real thing . . .
in America, anyway. Few people know this.
There are approximately 24,800 George Millers living in
our country. Half again that many are scattered throughout
the rest of the world. As with winter wheat and microproces-
sor chips, America produces the great bulk of the earth's sup-
ply of George Millers. (No one has yet suggested a workable
plan for exporting our surplus George Millers to Hungary or
the Sudan, two of the many nations where there are scarcely
any. And if you consider the literally countless Jorge Moli-
naros seeping into this country every year, a well-orchestrated
export program might do wonders for our balance of trade situation.)

No famous American answers to the name George Miller.
We have Arthur, Ann, and Henry Miller, and we had Glenn
Miller. We even have Beer, Miller. But no George Millers,
unless you give the benefit of the doubt to President Carter's
Treasury Secretary, Mr. G. William Miller, who simply may
be shy about being *the* George Miller, afraid of representing
alone all the other 24,799 less renowned George Millers.
Or it may be that our former Fed chairman's full name is
Gabby William Miller or *Grizzly* William Miller, and the
man is understandably reluctant to be the constant object of
newscasters' smirks and bankers' giggles.

America's 36,000 James Smiths would seem to be angling

for a purchase on the real thing of names. There is an official Jim Smith Society to which a hefty fraction of people named Jim Smith belong, that name being the sole prerequisite of membership. We should commend whichever Jim Smiths concocted the idea for their Society, since the formation of such a fraternity shows a keen appreciation for the joys of precision banality. But it also indicates they're trying too hard, like the girl in grammar school who wags and waves her raised hand to better catch the teacher's eye. Lobbying sometimes backfires.

George Miller is not even close to being the most common American name, but it is right up there in the top thirty or so. Every decent neighborhood should by odds contain at least one George Miller. Statistically, about one in nine thousand Americans is named George Miller, but your average community will have at least twice as many men called William Smith and Charles Jones. Indeed, all of those top-of-the-frequency-chart names sound as though they belong to personnel officers or black halfbacks. George Miller suffers less from these prejudices, being more the overweight Lutheran accountant type.

And the name George Miller has one singular nicety about it: it is a "prime name." Like prime *numbers* which cannot be reduced by division—not without a lot of trouble anyhow—prime *names* aren't subject to diminutives and nicknaming. John Smith has to contend with Jack Smith or even Smitty; Robert Johnson is reduced to Bobby J. overnight; and George Jones quickly becomes Jonesy, or divorced from Tammy Wynette. George Miller isn't easily hacked into a locker-room nubbin of its former self. Some insistent jerks—the kind of people who would have called Paul Robeson "Bubba"—will not be stopped: Georgie results, or GM, before long changed back to Georgie-Porgie, then Porgy, and finally Porg.

Were I the father of sons, and my last name Miller, I'd give my kid an indestructible name. It'd be either Max or D'Artagnan, depending on the mother's inclinations.

FESTIVALS

Holy Week (*or* "*La Semana Santa*") *in Seville, Spain*
is the real thing . . .
and it makes the notable contenders—the Newport Jazz, all
the Saints', the Woodstock, and the sundry Tuber Worship-
ping celebrations in peasant lands*—seem by comparison like
Clarence Wilson's birthday party in the third grade. The experience of a festival is resolutely subjective, and so I'm relying
now on the fact that La Semana Santa nearly spun this author (a child of haphazard Unitarians, a child who attended
an atheist Sunday school, sporadically) right into the bosom
of popish Christendom.

For us gimpy souls suckled on the pieties of insurance man
Protestantism, or even on the cloying mellowness of post-
Esalen American Catholicism, the spectacle of Spanish Holy
Week could make for some sure-fire apostasies. Spanish Catholicism during any week of the year is all hard muscle and
dignity. For the seven days preceding Easter, Sevillans play
for keeps.

This is not some TV-subsidized Mummers' gala or a noisy
Knights of Columbus prance down the avenue. It doesn't just
congest boulevards and back alleys for a few hours, or send

* I've always had the sneaking suspicion that all those colorful, joy-
ous Honduran harvest festivals were conceived and produced by bored
Peace Corps volunteers.

delirious firemen's children roaming about downtown for a blithe afternoon out of school. There are unending slow marches of *serious* penitents, in black cassocks and bare feet, each lugging two, three, and more thirty-pound crosses on his shoulders for the half-day trek to the cathedral. Every hundred-strong brotherhood of suffering marchers also carries two enormous polychrome sculptures—one of the Virgin and one of a bleeding Jesus—on its collective shoulders. Village bands play weeping dirges that sound nothing like "Raindrops Keep Fallin' on My Head" or "Hooray for the Irish." Gun-toting votaries of the young Franco walk in jackboot formation. No baton-twirlers in sight, but plenty of fried squid and dark wine. This quiet marathon frenzy goes on and on, and by the fifth night, when weird Moorish music skulks in the shadows, by God the incense begins to make sense.

CUTENESS

A *baby koala bear doing somersaults*
is the real thing . . .
which is not to say a thing to be encouraged. But spontaneous cuteness isn't so bad. It's contrived mass cuteness, rather, which afflicts us today. Items such as Goldie Hawn and docudramas about otter families and thematic "children's menus" and baby pictures with funny captions and all merchandise on which Charles Schulz receives a royalty are our scourge. These high-keyed distillates of true cuteness are to the real thing as saccharin is to sugar: artificial, probably cancer-causing, cosseted by underloved secretaries, and leaving of an annoying metallic aftertaste.

SITUATION COMEDIES

"*Green Acres*" (1965–71) was the real thing . . .
the consummate product of producer Paul ("The Beverly
Hillbillies" and "Petticoat Junction") Henning's neo-agrarian
comedy workshop.

Take a paper-dollar-thin premise, the goofier the better: your comedic *situation*. In "Green Acres" you had your
earnest city slicker, played by erstwhile *mensch* Eddie Albert;
and you had your bumble-brained overripe wife, played by the
bumble-brained overripe Eva Gabor. Call the middle-aged
lawyer *Oliver Wendell* Douglas. (Cute. And I guess they
couldn't name him Louis Dembitz Douglas.) Lawyer con-
tracts midlife crisis, decides to chuck Manhattan's bustle for
life on a farm. Fur-lined, martini-lapping spouse tags along,
reluctantly. And thus you have a *TV Guide* synopsis of an
early *Green Acres* episode: "Lisa (Eva Gabor) gets her first
look at the farm and, as far as she's concerned, one look is
enough!" And as far as we're concerned, that single sentence
is enough. It's a perfectly adequate summary of *every one* of
the show's 140 episodes, the best test of any situation comedy
worthy of the appellation.

But don't jump to reasonable conclusions: "Green Acres"
was not the worst comedy series ever broadcast on television.
"Gilligan's Island" and "My Mother the Car" ran closer to
that distinction, and a couple of the current prime-time min-

strel shows (e.g., "The Jeffersons") are arguably more horrible. "Three's Company," all things considered, is among the very worst in history.

But the producers of "Green Acres," Henning and a man named Jay Sommers, had that extra touch of shamelessness. Theirs was a downright lust for bizarre sit-com nonsense just this side of surrealism. It was empty-headedness run amok, cretins mainlining discount speed.

And how classic the video lineage of "Green Acres"! The show was a spin-off of another spin-off ("Petticoat Junction") of a rip-off ("The Beverly Hillbillies") of an imbecilic feature film (*Ma and Pa Kettle Go to Town*). (This is some brazen-faced feat, even for television. Overpraised Norman Lear, who's created more than *fifteen* sit-coms, only managed spin-offs of rip-offs (e.g., "Maude"). But he, along with Garry ("Happy Days") Marshall tends to milk at least two spin-offs from each original rip-off. When you get into permutations like rip-offs of second-generation spin-offs which are themselves first-generation rip-offs—such shows exist—the sense of *déjà vu* verges on the psychotic. Maybe network programming executives are spending too many hours in their offices fraternizing with office equipment; maybe Xerography is contagious.

But back to "Green Acres." Remember the jaunty theme song? Sing along!

> Green Acres is the place to be!
> Farm living is the life for me!
> Land spreading out so far and wide,
> Keep Manhattan, just gimme that countryside!

And people say there'll never be another Robert Frost. . . . But wait: the second stanza, a merry counterpoint by Miss Gabor, recalls the throbbing urban odes of William Carlos Williams.

New York is where I'd rather stay!
I get allergic smelling hay!
I just adore a penthouse view!
Darling I love you but give me Park Avenue!

And if you wanted stereotypes, it was stereotypes—dumb and unfunny—that "Green Acres" gave you. Lurking around as foils for Albert and Gabor were Tom Lester as Eb, the hideously inbred hillbilly defective; and hideously unbred Pat Buttram as the criminal, Mr. Haney. When "Green Acres" was canceled, so were several acting careers. (At the risk of seeming meretriciously serious, I find it noteworthy, albeit meaningless, that "Green Acres" ratings peaked and then declined precisely parallel with the intensity of our Indochina campaign.)

Occasionally, the late Edgar Buchanan and the even later Bea Benaderet—"Uncle Joe" and "Kate" of the siring series, "Petticoat Junction"—would pop into the "Green Acres" tableaux. (Needless to say, hilarious hijinx ensued.) We were meant to understand the Green-Beverly-Petticoat axis as a single, seamless TV universe. You could never be absolutely sure which of the three you were watching. In this sense we might regard creator Paul Henning as the Eli Whitney of American television production.

Soon we had the spectacle of "Gomer Pyle, U.S.M.C." oozing into "The Andy Griffith Show" and vice-versa. We have the same kinds of mongoloid Siamese twins—"Happy Days"/"Laverne and Shirley" and "Three's Company"/"The Ropers"—among the most popular series on television today, all threatening to sprout still more prime-time appendages. (We could even get Diff'rent Strokes: The Motion Picture.)

Just think of it: somewhere over that limpid blue TV horizon may lie an era when all television series fictively mate and intertwine. Barney Miller arrests the Fonz on a charge of statutory rape—Kristy McNichol is the victim—and he's defended in a feature story by Lou Grant. The piece is picked up by

"60 Minutes"—Mike Wallace asks rhetorically if street violence might not be the cause of mayhem on TV—and Archie Bunker is so enraged by the whole affair that he begs Jim Rockford to find Kristy's true attacker. Rockford, however, is away in Hooterville, masquerading as a grange executive at a reunion of the "Green Acres" crowd, all of whom are watching a Hallmark special, *Hal Holbrook Tonight!*, which stars Rich Little made up to resemble Holbrook. All are watching this one-man show, that is, except Ellie May Clampett, who's away on a "Love Boat" cruise with Gilligan (who keeps confusing Gavin MacLeod with Alan Hale, Jr.), and Eb, convicted three years earlier of burning a cross on the Jeffersons' terrace. Ratings, redux, and a cool subtext for the critics besides.

Big Sur, in California, is the real thing.
The hippies knew what they were doing this time. You'd ring up a successful investment banker to find the best corporate bonds, and a trucker is said to know where the best eats are. So when you want to know where to flee for a happy good time amid the flora and nicer fauna, ask a foot soldier of the U.S. counterculture (ret.).

A certain kind of person might write an Interior factotum and ask which is the most splendidly virginal parcel of nature under the Department's jurisdiction. Ah, Maine's sea-sprayed Arcadia! Ah, nearly the whole of the forty-ninth state! Ah, Minnesota's (and Canada's) Quetiquo Boundary Waters! Ah, still wilder wildernesses! Ah, the allure of trackless wastes: no toilets, no pajamas, and time aplenty for acute contemplation of bloody feet and the eldritch grunts and stirrings of animals after dark. Those are not places *to be:* they are places to know about, to maintain as our nation's psychic Eden, perhaps, and to save from defoliation by energy profiteers. But as vacation spots they're suited only for excessively fit graduate students and reclusive algae. Their scariness potential is just too high, and not outweighed by their scenic splendor coefficient.

Big Sur *is* a nice place to visit (but you surely wouldn't want to live there unless you're too young at heart and love nothing more than building meditation soddies). It's comfy. It's very, very pretty, but not numbingly beautiful. Around Big Sur we are seldom obliged to gasp and gasp again at God's mountain-moving wonders. Rather, this rolling, forested chunk of beachfront nature is something He tossed off in a few spare moments on Saturday evening. It's generous. It's copasetic.

Here are freshets gurgling agreeably through the luxuriant underbrush, and exuberant little waterfalls that seem to leap as much as fall, just to relieve the monotony of Big Sur's perfect hush. But the place is so damn fog-enshrouded so much of the time—fog time's when you disengage, slump up on Partington Ridge, and read a poor translation of Lao-tse by the dusky light pouring down through redwood latticework—you don't soon take the manifold succor for granted.

And then comes the jilting crispness of January afternoons in Big Sur, with the mist burned off altogether. You can sit amid the troops of bluff-topping cypress, and the wind off the Pacific pulls its punches like a sweet-tempered older brother. Clean sea smells and queer forest ones whirl around. It's all akin to an old Chinese rice-paper painting, cozy and expansive at the same time, never taking too many liberties or making too many demands. Stay there a spell longer; watch the sea lions frolic; no need to drive down to Bixby just yet; you've got time; Route One'll be emptier after six; sit. There is nothing you must do.

SCREENWRITERS

Elwood Ullman is the real thing.
"Elwood *who?*" the many will ask. ("*Who* Ullman?"
others may wonder. A simple "*What?*" might be the response
of still others.) How is it possible that an artist of singular accomplishment remains unknown to all but a few American
moviegoers? Even the most learned cinéastes know shame-
fully little about the particulars of Ullman's life and work.

You can keep Hecht and Loos and Schraeder and
Chayefsky. You can have your Dunnes, your Sargents, and all
your Goldmans. Ullman stands alone. At the rate of two a
year, every year, Elwood Ullman cranked out (and co-cranked
out) more than forty movie scripts. (By comparison, the famous American playwright Eugene O'Neill finished only
about twenty plays during his entire life, and they were
mostly real depressing.) The master of every movie genre but
the prisoner of none, Ullman represents the apotheosis of
Hollywood writers.

And perhaps finally no further biographical detail is required, for a straightforward inventory of Ullman's work is by
itself stark proof of the man's accomplishment. We stand
paralyzed before his incredible legacy, agog.

The Screenwriting Credits of Elwood Ullman:
A Partial Catalogue

Honeymoon Ahead
Ghost Catchers
Idea Girl
Men in Her Diary
Swingin' in the Corn
Susie Steps Out
The Stooge
Sailor Beware
Harem Girl
Ma and Pa Kettle On Vacation
Gold Raiders
Ma and Pa Kettle at Waikiki
Loose in London
Clipped Wings
Hot News
Paris Playboys
Bowery to Bagdad
Bowery Boys Meet the Monsters

Jungle Gents
Dig That Uranium
Jail Busters
Hot Shots
In the Money
Spook Chasers
Snow White and the Three Stooges
The Three Stooges Meet Hercules
The Three Stooges in Orbit
The Three Stooges Go Around the World in a Daze
The Outlaws Is Coming
Tickle Me
Dr. Goldfoot and the Bikini Machine
The Ghost in the Invisible Bikini

The MK 44 MOD O 550-pound Lazy Dog Missile Cluster
is the real thing . . .
although every American surely has his or her own favorite.
Heaven knows it's become chic to croon over the futuristic
deadliness of the Ingram M-10. A dozen-and-a-half rounds per
second is enough to make pacifists smile, and with a recoil no
more violent than a toddler's kick, the Ingram has the clean
sex appeal of the first pocket calculators.

It would be easy to single out the show-offy "smart bomb"
—GW Walleye Mark I in Pentagon lingo—as the state-of-the-
art real thing. You may have seen the future of war and its
name is Walleye Mark I, but the TV-guided smart bombs,
despite the spunky nickname, are wanting. Who could not
like the idea of television dispatching a missile with sniper precision to its target? (Perhaps moments before their annihi-
lation, those befuddled enemy hear Walter Cronkite's voice
from on high, "And that's the way it is—")

But waging a war (or even defensive incursions) by push-
button has no soul, no historical echoes. And that's one reason why our arsenal of nuclear megatonnage isn't even in the
running here. Mushroom beclouded havoc may be efficient
and all, but it sure isn't funky.

Think, rather, of primitive whoppers like the big half-ton
napalm bomb. Upon impact the napalm-laden MK 79 loses

its sheet-steel casing, and the area is flash-flooded with a hundred gallons of flame. These are the babies that made sizzling crypts out of so many Vietnamese burrows. Not quite a Spanish barkentine ablaze, maybe, but at least our incendiaries begin to resonate with schoolboy fantasies of war and weaponry.

In my book, the Lazy Dog Missile Cluster is the natural choice. First, the name of the thing is pure American. Don't tell me the military neologists aren't brilliant: they've coupled Uncle Remus ("Lazy Dog") with Dr. Strangelove ("Missile Cluster") and produced a pet name that must sound terrific drawled over the radio by some good ol' boy F-15 pilot out on a sortie.

Just like its name, the weapon itself is a mix-and-match combination of the brutally crude and the technologically with-it. It might have been designed by a wild-eyed child, scribbling in his social studies workbook. What does this jewel of extirpation do? It destroys only people, those who happen to be inside an area the size of a spacious two-bedroom apartment. The Cluster is dropped from a plane and in midair precisely over the target its smallish core of TNT detonates. The steel housing rips open and out fly ten thousand sharp iron spikes, not unlike the ten-penny nails Dad used to buy, all whizzing earthward at thousands of feet per second. Then everyone dies.

BEAUTIFUL PEOPLE

Bianca Jagger is, or was, anyway, the real thing . . .
for she's fading fast, seemingly cursed—like the concept she
epitomizes—with a pitilessly short shelf life. By the time these
words reach you she may be no more famous than Dean
Jagger's niece. These matters move quickly.

Bianca is many things to many people. To some she is so
much chaff from the accelerating celebrity gossip mill. For
others she is a delicate, dusky symbol of her times. And to
still others Bianca is a pocket-sized aerosol canister ideal for
surreptitious minty squirts during a date.

But what makes one a Beautiful Person in the decidedly
non-literal Liza-Andy-Truman sense? By this time there must
be plenty of little girls and boys in America who've chucked
the idea of becoming doctors or claims adjusters or assistant
photocopy coordinators. There must be kids who yearn to be
Beautiful People when they grow up (or, anyhow, when they
get older), children who'd rather read *W* than *My Weekly
Reader*. As a service to these well-tanned third-graders and
their still-aspiring parents, a preliminary self-help guide:

1) Have lunch with Arnold Schwarzenegger. Do not
have lunch with Sam Levenson, or with obviously hetero-
sexual Negroes.

2) Be (or at least know) a woman with one of the

following names: Chappy, Chessy, Lala, Muffy, Cece, Bambi, Nana, Caca, Doodoo, or Bobo.

3) The Duchess of Windsor, or whomever, was correct, as far as her famous dictum goes. But today's Beautiful Person can never be too thin, too rich, *or* too untalented.

4) Befriend two or more intellectuals, one of whom must be Arthur M. Schlesinger, Jr.

5) Design something, preferably a muted thing.

6) Considerably broaden your notion of what is "charming."

7) Tolerate with amused titters behavior among your peers which you would otherwise report to the police.

8) Do not serve Chee-tos to your dinner guests.

9) Don't get your hopes up about parenting anything but gracious ninnies. Better yet, don't have children at all. For their sake.

10) Chivalry may be dead, but sycophancy is not.

These commandments are tentative. Flexibility is paramount. If not for a remarkable social agility, what chance had a young Nicaraguan commoner—a girl of neither accomplishment nor means—for entry into the current edition of café society? Even though it remains an expanding vocational field, *beau monde* entry-level positions are scarce. And no one is born a Beautiful Person. This is important to remember.

When Bianca married Mick Jagger in 1971 she was almost automatically accorded probationary Beautiful Person status. Fortunately for her, those glittery nuptials coincided with the first signs of Mick's deft slide into the world of important grown-ups. Bianca could have ended up a pathetic ultragroupie or, only a little better, a burdensome professional partner. But Mick and Bianca were level-headed about her new role: she became an exotic ornament, an apparently devoted mother (to Jade, a far nicer name than China, Elijah Blue, god or Moon Unit), and a general smoother of rough edges.

It was her adoption by the couturier Halston that clinched it for Bianca. In Mick Jagger she'd struck gold; in Halston she found the man who could assay and refine her ore. Under his preening and tutelage, Bianca arrived (and stayed something of a star even after Mick decided against monogamy in favor of tall blondes relatively fluent in English).

Bianca has no significant achievements to her credit. Any number of women are more gorgeous than she, and even her sultry Third World allure has been done better. The *bons mots* aren't known to fly fast from her corner of the banquette. They say she has an ingratiating little-girl vulnerability, a quality only occasionally charming in little girls.

So why her? Why is Bianca by all accounts still a central member of 1980's batch of Beautiful People? Beats me. But I guess that's the point: if you have to ask, you can't afford it.

MYTHS ABOUT CHILDHOOD

That *all babies look like Winston Churchill*
is the real thing . . .
for if you look closely, you'll notice that no infant—in the
Northern Hemisphere, anyway—looks anything like Sir Winston. Rather, each is the spitting image of Neville Cham-
berlain. This may be the reason for babies' notoriously non-
aggressive behavior, why toddlers habitually rush to appease
mightier forces, such as their parents, pre-school supervisors,
and Axis Powers.

The conventional wisdom on childhood is riddled with
falsehoods. For instance:

> *The only thing any child desires is the unconditional
> love of his parents.*

This is sheer, self-serving arrogance on the part of mothers
and fathers. Most babies, in fact, want nothing more than a
comfortable income and some decently tailored clothing.
Studies have shown they only grudgingly tolerate the fondles
and coos, figuring their parents are the only people they know
well who might put them in touch with a good broker.

> *Children become homosexual as a result of domineering
> mothers and weak fathers.*

Nonsense. Three-year-olds *freely choose* a gay lifestyle, or not, depending upon how attractive they imagine they'd look in tight size 2 blue jeans and tiny leather bomber jackets. (Children have been in a few cases "turned gay" by a homosexual pet, such as a cat. All cats are gay, or at least put an unsavory premium on good posture and tidiness.)

Children raised in a family which prizes reading, conversation, and unbridled curiosity will be intellectually superior adults.

How easily we are deceived. New studies have shown that it is not parental *attitudes,* but rather a child's *physical* environment which makes for future intellectual success. In one experiment, the home of an illiterate ghetto teen-ager—his parents both alcoholic book-burners—was redecorated with masses of hanging plants, exposed brick walls, Chagall prints, and Shaker furniture. Within a year, "X" (not his real name) was an honors student at Yale and a contributor to *The Nation.*

Parents should read aloud to their children at bedtime.

This is a double lie. First of all, studies have shown that it's far more beneficial for parents to read *silently* to their kids. How better to encourage a sturdy self-reliance and an insatiable curiosity? Secondly, a child's bedtime is not good for any child-rearing activity, since children are always drifting off at some inconvenient hour, an hour when you'll want to be out on the town, squandering the kids' college education money at night clubs and gaming houses.

PRESIDENTIAL PRIVILEGES

The CIA's map and chart service is the real thing . . . and informed sources say it's the one Jimmy truly cherishes, too. Carter *loves* maps and charts, their clean, quantitative purity being just the thing to perk up a former naval officer/ engineer/food wholesaler. I discovered some months ago that the CIA spends between three and five thousand dollars *every day* preparing maps and charts for the President's security briefings. It would take quite a number of AAA Trip-Tiks to expend twenty thousand a week. It's a shame that only the President gets to look at the little blue dots indicating the number of armored battalions massed on the Zimbabwe border. And I'll bet he gets a neat new plastic overlay every morning, too, the lucky dog.

The only competition in this category—the power to wage nuclear war—cannot fairly be counted as a strictly *Presidential* option. It is, rather, a divine prerogative which our highest elected official temporarily assumes along with the power to name August 9 National Toaster Safety Day. (And while we're on the subject, we'll see true democracy in this country only when each and every *citizen* has the right to dispatch ICBMs to Russia, with a Button on every American mantelpiece and every family its own Joint Chiefs of Staff, Grandma and the little kids getting a half vote each.)

PLANETS

Neptune is the real thing . . .
for obvious reasons. And if you know what's good for you and
civilization as you know it, you'll take my word for it. Incidentally, if intelligent life should be found to exist on other
worlds—Neptune, say—be assured that those creatures are benign and cute, just like Robin Williams and Ray Walston
and the aliens in *Close Encounters*. Really quite friendly
beings if you don't make disparaging remarks about the am-
monia odor, or make any statements requiring even a basic
grasp of Cartesian logic. Very courteous folk. Except they
grant no quarter to troublemakers who become hysterical or
notify the Strategic Air Command or anything like that.
They mean you no harm, should they exist. Really. Just don't
panic.

LABOR UNIONS

*The International Association of Machinists and
Aerospace Workers*
is the real thing . . .
and the IAMAW is further distinguished by a president who
bears the funniest name of any person in public life. Wimpy
Winpisinger is the leader of the IAMAW—a tough, independent and suitably foul-mouthed labor man, his toy name
notwithstanding.

I am ordinarily a strong advocate of judging books by their
covers, but judging trade union leaders by their names is
wrong. He often seemed unpleasant, but close friends say
George *Meany* really wasn't one, and I. W. *Abel* wasn't very,
as president of the United Steelworkers. And I've heard nothing to suggest that the former chief of the United Auto
Workers—Leonard *Woodcock*—is fitted out with a prosthesis
of any kind aside from his smile.

A lot of people will argue that if a union's president hasn't
been kidnaped and made into secret mulch, then his union
has no right being called the real thing. But they are wrong:
there's far more to running a union than dipping into a pension fund and making enormous unsecured loans to friends
with Italian surnames.

Indeed, William "Wimpy" Winpisinger is easily as honest
as the handsome drones who employ his members. He has

called some of his own ideas socialist; yet in 1979 his union argued before the Supreme Court that Wimpy had a right to purge commie troublemakers from the ranks. He has called the sitting Democratic President "an asshole" and "a little fink." Wimpy is a great man.

His is the least familiar of the Big Unions. You don't often hear Barbara Walters reporting on "secret jawboning sessions between the Labor Secretary and labor chieftain Wimpy Winpisinger." But the IAMAW with its membership of almost a million genuine *workers* is either the fourth or fifth largest union in America, the rank depending on whether you count the teachers' truly wimpy National Education Association as a real union.* I'll bet Wimpy doesn't.

* The following organizations were disqualified, it might be charged unjustly, because they aren't "real": The American Federation of Steamship Vandalizers, the United Lactose Workers, the International Association of Velvet Mongers, the Independent Tungsten Haulers Union, and the Kindling Choppers' Benevolent Association.

WOOD

Oak is the real thing . . .
because mahogany and good old chestnut too willingly become veneer, because walnut's appeal depends so much on
flashy stumpwood burls, and because it's sad to think about
quiet, lithe birch trees being ripped into planks by a 36-inch
saber-saw.

Red cedar is a faddish California upstart and more than deserves its status as the favorite of pot-smoking, stockbroking
sauna builders, a peg or two beneath white cedar's solid performance as the blanket chests of great-aunts everywhere.

(Did you know that until its recent sprouting in sunny
American soils, *true* cedar had its roots exclusively in war-torn
underdeveloped nations? Yes: the Himalayas, North Africa,
Cyprus, and Lebanon were the only lands on earth the true
cedar called home.)

Teak and ebony are just too precious. Redwoods are freaks.
Balsa is retarded. Rosewood is too womanish, and maple—
sugar maple, anyway—too manly. Pine is prosaic, fine for pil-
ings and fenceposts but nothing you'd invite to a party. Elm
is a simp: if it isn't felled by disease while living, it bends and
warps in death. Sycamore may fool you at first, but it's a
sickly brother-under-the-bark to elm. And it's a chore to take

seriously the lunatic fringe like primavera, and fiddlebacked sandalwood. We're grownups here.*

In cherry you've a venerable beauty. From George Washington's naughty boyhood chopping, to Chekhov's idyllic grove, to the dark, patrician slabs covering the walls of the library in your own fabulously expensive home, cherry is a graceful wood indeed. But one doesn't *build* things from cherry wood. You make a desk or a pretty armoire, but that's not the same as *building*.

The great masted ships were built of groaning half-ton oaken timbers. Parts of Westminster Abbey are oak from a time when the Domesday Book was taught in current-events classes, and the beams stand sturdy after nine centuries of damp, fire, buzz-bombs, and smog. The quartersawed oak floorboards in colonial parlors still throw off a hard and stubborn gleam.

The wood of the oak is unquestionably great. But you also have a far-flung family of oak trees. There's the luscious decadence of the South's live oaks, a young Snopes boy straddled over that high limb there, tossing mumblety-peg and humming "Dueling Gene Pools" to himself. Or a Massachusetts Lowell puttering with his moral character in the shade of a fat white oak. Or a happy son in Adidas, Ohio, hammering away at a tree house in the boughs of that old red oak in his backyard. And yet for all that, oaks seem to go under the saw happily, born to please humans like Li'l Abner's Shmoos.

* Speaking of oddballs, there's plywood, the Frankenstein monster of the lot. Plywood is Arizona's state tree, but despite repeated pleas from the governor of that state, I've chosen not to consider it here. I even sent back the genuine Indian turquoise pen-and-pencil set and the Goldwaters' gift certificate.

IMPRESSIONISTS

Claude Monet is the real thing . . .
as everyone knows. See? Sometimes plain common sense and
the conventional wisdom are correct, even in this tricky quest
for the quintessential. After all, you can only stretch a nuance
so far. At some point in time, you have to leave the belabored
distinctions to the Ron Zieglers of the world. Monet's the
one, obviously.

Monet, who died just a year before Charles Lindbergh
touched down near his home,* was for practical purposes the
founder of Impressionism and its stubborn troop leader for
several decades. His artistic policies were simple and sensible.
Claude Monet wanted to paint *what he saw,* literally, not
what the orderer or the charlatan in him told him he ought to
see, and paint. He didn't set up his easel in front of Chartres
and endeavor to paint a "cathedral." No: Monet saw a shim-
mering plane of pale blue there in the window, and he
painted a dab of pale blue; jagged streaks of aqua shadow
flecked with orange light, he painted the aqua and dappled on
the orange. There are no crazy juxtapositions of light and
form and color in Monet's alarmingly bright paintings, no

* Monet died just a scant year *after* the Treaty of Locarno was
signed, and nearly *six* years *before* Charles Lindbergh, Jr. was kidnaped. Thus we may completely rule out Monet either as a cause of
the Second World War or as the murderer of Lindbergh's baby. The
debate over Bruno Hauptmann's Impressionist "leanings" still rages.

impossible collages of breasts and noses and guitars. Monet strove to paint a beaming picture of the scene as it looked in the E.P.N. (Eternally Present Now). It's not nearly as simple as this, of course, but my business here is to make long stories unconscionably short. And so painting what was seen, no more or less, became an ism.

To mention Monet is to conjure up images of nature, naturally. But he never pined for the rustic, for the raw and unspoiled. Monet preferred his nature tamed and civilized. The sun and sky and water were lovely, just so long as there was a cool bistro a short walk away, across the meadow (and, mostly, outside the canvas). A pleasant lunch of pâté and pernod always helps keep those Impressions flowing. Crazy Paul Gaugin—*synthetism?* Are you kidding or what?—he could grab a rucksack and head for the jungle, but uh-uh, I'll catch you later, *mon ami;* the boulevard beckons. (M. Monet wouldn't be distressed to know that a square yard of his goods —signed, framed, plus tax and commissions—goes today for $300,000, easy.)

Why do we all like Impressionist works so much? Because our souls are given more sustenance than a mean contemplation of surface, surface, *surface.* These are no "painted words." We don't glance at an Impressionist's painting and harrumph that our kid sister/four-year-old son/pet chimp could've painted that . . . *thing.* (It's not until long after the turn of the century and the work of those nutty Abstract Expressionists that we're really tempted to put peevish inflectional quotation marks around "art," as in, "You call that *'art'?"*)

Impressionism was the last thoroughly legitimate flowering of pictures. That is a train station. Those are water lilies. That is a footbridge over a river and those are pretty girls with parasols on the bank. Impressionist paintings may be a trifle fuzzy—or even composed entirely of thousands and thousands of fuzz bits—and the pure colors aren't always *exactly* true to life. But we understand art sufficiently well to approve of these reasonable mutations, as long as they come from the heart.

You probably know more than you know you know about art, even if you think you only know what you like. Like Monet.

TAX SHELTERS

Marrying an Irish artist is the real thing . . .
although it certainly implies a level of commitment—an aching hunger to deprive the IRS—that buying a limited partnership in a Tulsa shopping center, for example, does not. On the other hand, you can't take your one per cent interest in a K-Mart home to meet the folks.

Contrary to populist imagery, a tax shelter doesn't have to be anything so exotic as a cattle-buying cabal, or motorcycle movies financed with money leveraged four-to-one. A tax shelter is simply any one of hundreds of legal maneuvers by which portions of your income are made exempt from taxes. Having a kid is a tax shelter—a foolish one, even if the birth can be arranged for the last week of December, since the long-term cost of operating a child far exceeds the shelter it provides. Municipal bonds are tax shelters. The personal pension plans (Keogh and IRA, the latter unrelated to Ireland or its artists) are tax shelters. Anything that harbors your income from taxation is a tax shelter.

The complex syndicated non-recourse convertible partnership depreciation schemes give a few people—high-rolling dentists, gullible movie stars and clever heiresses, mostly—a way to beat the feds unavailable to the average Joe, he resigned to ranting about decimated take-home pay. But in their Byzantine abstraction lies most shelters' problem: no gut satisfaction, no fine thrill of taking personal action to stump the bastards. You want your dodge to be anecdotal. You want to be able to tell your chums, "I did this simple thing, and because of it, *they can't get me*."

What's more concrete and personal than getting married? Getting hitched to an ordinary American is in some cases a sort of tax shelter: if you make lots more money than your spouse, you file a joint tax return, and he or she effectively becomes a tax shelter. But that's a primitive tax lean-to compared to the scam available by wedding the right foreigner.

Irish artists and writers can get immunity from their country's taxes. (Even some *non-*Irish writers and artists living in Ireland can escape tax liability under the romantic fools' policies, but that's another story.) If you marry an Irish artist, *half* your income is legally his or hers, assuming the right community-property laws apply. So if you earn forty thousand dollars a year, twenty thousand of that sum is considered your mate's legal share. And if that half-share is the share of a non-resident alien, the non-resident alien owes no American taxes on it. And if that non-resident alien is also an Irish artist exempt from Irish taxes, the scheme is glistening perfection. No more corned-beef-and-spud dinners for you two. The hitch is that you, or at least your creative spouse, will be obliged to spend great quantities of time in the Irish Republic every year. But who knows? Maybe you could cover County Cork with tax-sheltered singles apartments and make enough so that you can afford to divorce that cranky Irish spouse-of-convenience.

Spending the months of March and April in your big
villa somewhere in southern Spain
is the real thing . . .
far, far better for what ails you than pulling your own strings,
looking out for number one, or swallowing megadoses of Vi-
tamin B derivatives. As long as Vivaldi's on the hi-fi and
there's a pert Andalusian servant girl fetching my juice, I'm
a loving, giving, sharing, helping creature.

There are myriad ways to achieve contentment that don't
involve reading a small book with large print written by a
chipper man with an M.Ph.Ed. degree from Back of the Gun
Magazine Extension University. Here are a few of them:

1. Keep away from people with a rosy glow of vigorous
self-confidence. They are the ones who by a process of
negative osmosis make you feel in need of emotional
redecorating. While all it is you really require is a new
shower-head and some sun, they'll soon have you building a whole new you.

2. Phone your parents collect and tell them you're
throwing in the towel: they were absolutely right, you
never will amount to anything without their help, and
you're moving back home. Having to be in bed with the
lights *out* by midnight is a small price to pay for true
emotional security. And getting tucked in is nicer than

getting drunk with some leering computer programmer, anyway.

3. Have an idea for a simple-but-indispensable invention, patent it, and make millions in royalties.

4. If you've spent all your recent weekends strolling through the South Bronx, visiting tornado victims' widows, watching Bangladesh travelogues, touring state asylums and loitering in hospital emergency rooms—*stop it this instant*. You'll be surprised at how quickly your outlook brightens up.

5. Start figuring your age in reverse cat years. How old are you? "I'm seven," you'll answer cheerfully, "in reverse cat years." Presto! No more obsession with approaching death, no more embarrassment about admitting your middle age. Some odd stares from new acquaintances, perhaps, but don't let those bother you: that's what good mental health is all about.

The *telephone company* is the real thing.

From the moment Alexander Graham Monopoly invented the device, the Bell system has been the only game in town. (All of which illustrates, by the way, how absurdly simple it would be to produce a book such as this in most of the Slavic nations, for instance, where the "real" and "only" things are conveniently synonymous.)

HOMOSEXUALS

Bert and Ernie, of "Sesame Street,"
are the real thing . . .
and that the two Muppets don't flaunt their gayness—Big
Bird is far swishier, and an old bitch besides—is very much
to the point. Bert and Ernie conduct themselves in the same
loving, discreet way that millions of gay men, women, and
hand puppets do. They do their jobs well and live a splendidly settled life together in an impeccably decorated cabinet.

In fact, Bert and Ernie lead a far more "normal" life than
bilious heteros like Cookie Monster and Grover. Nor for
these two lovers does the gay life have any connection with
the sad wrinkle-room existence of aging fairies such as Captain Kangaroo's Dancing Bear and Fran's Kukla.

Among theater folk today, as everyone is aware by now,
being homosexual is thought no more bizarre than having a
foam-rubber head, a two-dimensional face, or strings perma-
nently attached to one's limbs. None of Bert's and Ernie's
professional colleagues treat them oddly, in short, because
gayness is just another friendly part of life on "Sesame
Street." Why do you think you've never seen *Mrs.* Hooper?

Sweetbreads are the real thing . . .
and are (not coincidentally) the one part of himself that that
ex-steer would really prefer you didn't eat.

It is widely and wrongly believed that sweetbreads are cattle minds, but brains are called brains in beefdom. Others incorrectly believe sweetbreads to be bovine pancreas. An unu-
sually fluent waiter will tell you that they're the animal's
thymus glands. This isn't quite right either, since the thymus
is not a gland, strictly speaking, but a "gland-*like* structure."
Why quibble? And it really wouldn't do to order the shrimp
cocktail to start and, oh, I guess I'll have the braised gland-
like structures *à la Béarnaise*.

In man the thymus does something extremely important—
nobody knows just what or how—until childhood ends, when
the slippery clod of tissue tucked behind the collarbone turns
as vestigial as the Hippocratic Oath. We can only assume
that the calf's thymus is mysteriously critical to him, too.

Weird meats, according to our parents, either taste like
"chicken, sort of" or "you'll enjoy it," a phrase meaning
"liver" in High Parent. Sweetbreads don't have the flavor of
frogs' legs, rabbit, squid, or any of the low-down cattle innards. Euphemism encases sweetbreads like a cloudy white
membrane. They, along with stomachs, hearts, kidneys,

brains, and tongues are called *"variety* meats," despite the old adage that "variety is the tripe of life."

It's only fair to admit that I've fudged a bit: sweetbreads probably ought to be the real thing among *civilized* meats. Still, there is something willfully brutal about snatching a beast's glands for food. Who but the truest carnivore would delight in such a specifically bestial tidbit?

Yet for the true and pure in meat of the "me rip skin from snorting creature" kind, go directly to your local outlet of the Deer 'n' Brew chain (or Venison 'n' *Vin,* east of the Allegheny). Hot, dripping Bambi-flesh may disquiet the Cuisinart consciousness, but the sweet/rancid flavor of venison, déclassé or not, has no equal for absolute meatishness. (And for budget-minded consumers, dinner for a month can be snared by some reckless high-speed driving through a nearby national park at dusk.)

Sweetbreads have none of venison's gamy snarl. And though the icky *idea* of sweetbreads puts off many ordinary beef eaters, a bite of nicely blanched cow thymus has none of steak's unsettling string, gristle, and fat. Sweetbreads are polite: they don't go out of their way to remind you that you're chewing part of a previously living, mooing thing.

Sweetbreads raw look like some omnivorous prehistoric moth, two loaves of slipperiness connected by a nut of tubes and tissue (the more quickly cut away and less said about, the better). Cudgeled flat and decently cooked, sweetbreads are tamed into palatability. Hot and smooth, they are a tasteful beige color throughout, and sweetbreads taste as beige as they look. The frail, mushroomy taste nearly floats right past the tastebuds. Yet when they're served in a certain way to a diner in just the right mood, steamy sweetbreads can taste ominously, primordially familiar. Such flickerings of kinship are best suppressed with another glass of wine.

HAIKU

Haiku is the ancient Japanese poetic form in which the first line contains five syllables, the second seven syllables, and the last line five again. The word "haiku" translates literally as "amusing sentence"; the Japanese are noted for their love of the enigmatic and even, as in this case, of the boldfaced lie. You will be amused by most haiku only if you enjoy a good guffaw at the thought of lichen under cloudless skies.

The haiku form, generically, is also a real thing. Of precisely *what* it is the apotheosis remains unclear, but it seems to have something to do with private calligraphy lessons and moody little girls with foreign first names. Here, anyhow, is the true haiku, published for the first time anywhere:

> *Horrid, yellow grubs*
> *Colonizing my rice bowl:*
> *Elders' knowing smirks.*

At progressive schools, the kind that offer special bounties for the recruitment of mulatto children, students are forced to compose haiku in fulfillment of their Creative Behavior requirement. This is dangerous: if you allow children to believe they can write lyric poetry, before you know it they'll contract tuberculosis, drown, or both. Rather, children should be encouraged to invent seventeen-syllable advertising slogans.

Those attending progressive schools might be permitted to write their jingles in Japanese. (In any case it ought to be illegal for a child to possess any writing instrument other than a pencil at least one half inch in diameter, which pencil may be used exclusively to draw wobbly suns with flagellar rays, and Nazi airplanes dropping bombs on long-division problems.)

Certain non-Japanese adults will experience an urge to write haiku because "it's so nice and *simple*," and they will better spend their free time yodeling out the back door. If they still have hours to kill and pen in hand, a few might safely be given the go-ahead to write a sonnet in which the phrases "those treads are *suicide*, mister" and "a summer's day" appear prominently.

Maria Callas was the real thing . . .
though this isn't intended as mushy fag-hag eulogy. And let's
make one thing clear: opera is a basically alien life form to
both of us.

With the spate of celebrity deaths over the last few years,
that of Maria Callas was lost in the shuffle of intensive media
mourning. Even if she'd had a gaudy estate in Memphis (or
Scorpios) and performed to the end, lubricated with uppers
and fried peanut butter; if her remains had been swiped; if
there'd been a gigolo stenographer left wanting; or even if
she'd had a trillion dollars, Callas wouldn't have rated major
coverage. Maria Callas' demise was not fated to receive, in
these times, the phenomenal mawk that attended the pass-
ings of Elvis, Chaplin, the Duke, Groucho, or der Bingle. But
in the 1950s pop stardom surrounded Callas as it did almost
no one else. She was harassed by swarms of cameramen,
pricked by reporters of every nation, and given yards of col-
umn inches by the likes of Cholly Knickerbocker and Earl
Wilson. The hungry glare of press attention focused—yes!—
on an *opera* singer. Nothing like it since Caruso, and nothing
like it since. Imagine a female Travolta with genius and style.
Beverly Sills's neighborly fame doesn't even come close.

Nor should it. Here and there Sills and Sutherland were
Callas' technical superiors, it's true. But nobody has the

flaming zealousness of expression that Callas flaunted, nor her intensity at every pinpoint across a (nearly) three-octave range. As Bellini's Norma, as Anna Bolena, or Violetta in *Traviata*, she drove audiences to frenzy. With Callas the mad Lucia, people were deeply frightened.

In the end, Callas was Muhammad Ali to everyone else's Floyd Patterson. Maria Callas was this century's single *soprano assoluta*, and that's about all there is to it.

But riding shotgun with her instinctual talent was Callas' electric presence, offstage and on. (It wasn't her fault she looked like an emotionally disturbed Long Island housewife who'd been told all her life she's the spitting image of Audrey Hepburn.) The devalued word "charisma" has some rare meaning applied to Callas, and we can forgive the lady's pathological self-confidence. In fact it's just that sort of baroque, almost idiotic arrogance which seems a major ingredient of opera's spiritual fuel. "I'm the only one who has the nerve to do things right," she said, even in the face of rare but atrocious slipups. Like opera itself, Callas was audacious, majestic, ridiculous, emotional, misunderstood, risky, demanding, and, in the main, foreign.

Especially now at a time when popular images of Greekness are burdened with greasy "Cheeseburger, cheeseburger, Pepsi!" buffoons, or Anthony Quinn's interminable movie incarnations, the example of Maria Callas recalls that Real Things can exist unequivocally.

The *Collegiate Personality Quiz,* which appears below for the first time, is the real thing, designed by two famous psychologists whose names you'd recognize in an instant. These are the sorts of things that magazines like *Cosmopolitan, Seventeen,* and *Redbook* tuck fetchingly between penny-wise new mock guacamole recipes and fiction about ovaries. The quizzes are the best parts of many journals in which they appear. (Indeed, I was on the verge of canceling my subscription to *Glamour* until they began running more pieces like "Do You Need Distemper Shots? A Quick Quiz Tells You" and "The Get-Up-And-Go Test: Too *Much* Pep Can Be Hazardous".)

And we've all had the unhappy experience of sitting in our thanatologist's waiting room, flipping through a year-old issue of *Bland Living* or *The Journal of Funny Diseases.* Then, the teasing discovery of what looked to be an educational-yet-stimulating quiz—but with the answers already ticked off by some previous examinee.

Here, at last, you have a self-help quiz—the ultimate example of the genre—right in your very own book. It's untouched and pristine and begging you to take it yourself, *right now.*

But as you work your way through the questions, remember the advice proffered in the preface of every such quiz: "There are no 'right' or 'wrong' answers." This is true. There are no right or wrong answers, only desirable and undesirable people. Pencils ready? Begin.

1. Do you believe that book learning is all there is to life?

_____yes_____no

2. Do you own more Motown albums than you know black people?

_____yes_____no

3. When you pass a withered derelict slumped in a doorway, is your first impulse to reach for your Nikon?

_____yes_____no

4. Do you know what a Nikon is?

_____yes_____no

5. Is your pop a big success?

_____yes_____no

6. Do you watch as many game shows as a housewife who loves them because you hate them?

_____yes_____no

7. Do you chat about contraceptive jellies to persons of the opposite sex with whom you are barely acquainted?

_____yes_____no

8. Do you make a habit of going to working-class bars to establish solidarity with people not as good as yourself?

_____yes_____no

9. Do you frequently announce your intention to "go climbing this weekend"?

_____yes_____no

10. MEN: Do you read Gaelic folklore to make yourself more attractive to women?

_____yes_____no

11. WOMEN: Do you prefer anorexia to make-up?

_____yes_____no

12. Do you consider the salient question not *if* the world owes you a living, but how comfortable a one?

_____yes_____no

13. Do you wish your apartment building held its own pep rallies, so that you could neglect to go?

_____yes_____no

14. Do you do your thing and I do my thing?

_____yes_____no

14a. Are we in this world to live up to each other's expectations?

_____yes_____no

14b. If by chance we find each other, is it beautiful?

_____yes_____no

15. Do you choose your restaurants according to how late they're open rather than the quality of their food?

_____yes_____no

16. Do you pepper your conversation with the word "Zen" to camouflage your irresponsibility?

_____yes_____no

17. To appear cultured, yet a Regular Guy, do you drink Bass ale, wear L. L. Bean clothes, and pretend familiarity with generators?

_____yes_____no

18. Do you sometimes get this really weird feeling that you're *inside* like some M. C. Escher drawing and you can't, you know, escape?

_____yes_____no

19. Do you envy Dick Cavett more than you do Mick Jagger?

_____yes_____no

20. Are you *always* up for a heated-yet-reasoned discussion of current affairs?

_____yes_____no

21. Aren't you glad you use dialectics? Don't you wish everybody did?

_____yes_____no

SCORE YOURSELF: If you have even a trace of the collegiate in you, you outsmarted this quiz at the beginning, deducing that the "yes" response was the preferable choice, whether or not it was true in your case. So, as in all things collegiate, it matters not so much whether you do something well or badly, but how you get out of doing it honestly.

RACES

The black race is the real thing . . .
since none of the other human races really have much "onto-
logical salience" (a phrase I heard first [and last] used by a
philosophy major, black, who graduated *cum laude* from a
prestigious northeastern university and whose father was a
former loan shark and current master of origami).

Consider the standard clause of modern legal equality:
". . . *shall not discriminate on the basis of race, creed, color,
sex, or national origin.*" Now what that really means is that a
school or employer may not discriminate on the basis of being
black, odd, black, female, or probably black, respectively. The
sentence may read and work better in the more general form,
but it's black people who are being given their formal due.
That's salience.

For instance, it's usually not loitering groups of Chinese
men who are randomly set upon by police. Although they
have evolved some winning cultures in their time, Asians are
not notable for their racial pizzazz. And in all important re-
spects, the white race(s) are an anemic Bauhaus subcategory
of Asiatic. There being no question that whiteys lack soul, we
also come out poorly in the mysterious stoicism department.
(Except, typically, in one narrowly literal sense, since there's
such a section in every American bookstore, right between the
Media Studies and New Age Health shelves.)

No, Eldridge Cleaver convinced me long ago, back when he'd only been born once, that the white race had pathetically little to recommend it as a race *per se*. Its consolation of course, is the pleasant array of fringe benefits: decent schools, equal opportunity, harpsichord music, and never having to wear dashikis. Still, it would be a dreamy pleasure one day to be called "my man" or "bro'" by someone who wasn't trying to sell me drugs, or worse.

(For those of you expecting something entirely different from this chapter, the answers are the 800-meter run, at least in men's events; the Talladega 500; the Space; and the Preakness.)

Scorpio is the real thing . . .
and though "Whatsyoursign?" is no longer the modish in-
dicator of dumbness it was once, horoscopic narcissism still
gives the Holy Trinity a run for its money in the hearts and
minds of American seekers. They have little else commonly
denominating their wispy lives, but the waifish Cambridge
mime and the size 14 Missouri housewife and the swinging
foam salesman on the Coast all know about Neptune rising
and rationality descending.

Scorpios are people born between October 24 and Novem-
ber 21, and conceived, likely as not, on Groundhog Day. But
the important astrological feature of Scorpios is that more
than any other sign, they take their Scorpion origins seriously.
Scorpios are predisposed to a faith in astrological truth, a natural bent exceeded among the dozen other signs only by Pis-
ceans, who are generally too depressed to bother.

Your fascination with things astrological may be limited to
keeping tight hold on purse-strings today, and heeding advice
of a loved one who is far away, the daily funny-page portents
passing in and out of your data-soaked mind quicker than
Andy Capp's punchline. Scorpios require both less and more
than the rest of us. On one hand, every Scorpio might just as
well use the same dog-eared Jeane Dixon forecast, day after
day: "Spend every waking moment," the daily advice would

read, "unearthing hidden, seemingly deep meanings where others see only the routine and unremarkable."

While you and I may take pleasure in finishing the new Herman Wouk book, or in successfully completing a night course in massage for ponies, Scorpios get their purest epistemological kicks from long hours spent divining vaporous symbols and signs. You worry about the mortgage on the new house; Mr. Scorpio's bedeviled by what the hell Saturn and Neptune are doing together in his twelfth house. The true Scorpio finds our stiff world of parliaments, carburetor ratios, and RSVPs baffling at best. Who has time to consider a nephew's angel-dust addiction or unpaid telephone bills when there are natal aspects to calculate, midnight ephemerides to consult?

And as oxymoronic as it sounds, Scorpios are the occult's skeptics. They require reams of supporting evidence. They'll accept generosity from a Leo (Leos, the charts reveal, are *supposed* to be magnanimous) but never from a Capricorn. Astrology gives Scorpios tools for their credulity.

Dispassionate analysis aside, Scorpios' peculiarly astrological temper is the finest argument for preventive detention I've heard in years. Lock 'em up pending further outbursts of West Coastishness, or until the space shuttle program gets going and all the world's Scorpios can be manifested aboard for a one-way junket beyond the ozone, they closer to those all-revealing celestial bodies and we on earth a little bit happier with our clunky feet of clay.

REMINDERS OF THE 1960S

The town of Woodstock, New York, is the real thing . . . despite the more visible examples of the Grateful Dead's longevity, Elizabeth Swados, coed dormitories, body hair, and the word "lifestyle."

Woodstock is barely one hundred miles north of New York City, but this once-rustic arts colony is a Land That Time Forgot. Nineteen sixty-seven exists whole here. Before the end of the century, the state tourism authorities will be able to market Woodstock as an Aquarian Williamsburg. Vacationers will pay six dollars to tour a working tie-dye shop and sit in on mock sessions of the communal farm's weekly "Vibe Exchange." Others can watch actors, all dressed in artful reproductions of hippie clothing, smoke ersatz hashish and talk about dolphins' souls. There will be painstakingly rebuilt "crash pads," and mimes giving away free carob cookies from the back of a bright purple school bus. And at sunset every day (at least in season), all the visitors will assemble around the village green to witness a scaled-down re-creation of the Kent State killings, and a multimedia "teach-in" on the history of the activist era. Whole families will flock to see it all, tourist trap or not. ("Look, Adam, over there," graying Dad will say. "Now there's how your mom and I used to dress long before you were born." Little Adam, forbearing but bored by fatherly reminiscences, will beg to be taken through the black-light poster museum for the third time.)

Woodstock of the present moment is easy to imagine, and perhaps you've seen one of its less formidable copies which thrive up and down the Pacific coast. For Woodstock, take a town whose basic physical plant is an insubstantial reworking of the standard-issue New England town (see p. 53). Lay over that peeling clapboard base a turn-of-the-century immigration of well-meaning amateur landscape painters and utopian potters. Splash on a second wave, mid-century, of folk singers, rock musicians, and their stubborn tribes of hangers-on. And then to bring your mental picture entirely up-to-date, add a coterie of successful sandal entrepreneurs, burned-out recording engineers, incense and bhang merchants who got in on the ground floor. I don't know where have all the flowers gone, but the people who sold them have retired to Woodstock en masse.

Stores in Woodstock still have names like The Floating Ego and Naked Afternoon. One broker of land calls his agency Surreal Estate. It's not unusual for grade-school children to attend group-therapy sessions, and not out of the question for infants to diagnose their parents' karmic ills. There is no enterprise in Woodstock that does not sell sprouts: not just on salads and sandwiches—they dip your ice cream cone in alfalfa sprouts instead of chocolate sprinkles. Woodstock doctors prescribe mungbean shoots rather than aspirin. They put a satchel of greasy sprouts in your glove compartment when they fix your car, sprout tea is a staple, sprouts are used for clothing in some parts of town, and there exists an emergent Woodstock School of kinetic beansprout art.

Nursing mothers in the area breast-feed their children carrot juice. Folks have pickup trucks, some even equipped with back-of-the-cab gunracks—in which are secured magic wands, wooden recorders, and divining rods rather than Marlin semiautomatics. The town has more art galleries than American cars, and wing-tip shoes are illegal. The Holocaust is conceptualized as "the first holistic approach to murder."

But Woodstock is changing. It used to be that no one talked about "summering" in Woodstock. And there are the apocalyptic murmurs about a coming condominia blight. Once upon a time, playing Frisbee with your dog—and losing —was the closest thing to organized sport in Woodstock. Now empty meadows become tennis courts. No one yet keeps score ("too linear") but tennis is being played, and more than one ex-ex-jock has been spotted on the fairways at the Woodstock Country Club. The caddies carry the dope (but it's cool if they get high, too).

Change comes slowly. There are still a lot of gentle people here, and if you're coming, be sure to wear some flowers in your hair, or at least have them hanging from the rearview of your BMW.

LIMERICKS

A vice most obscene and unsavoury
Holds the Bishop of Balham in slavery:
With maniacal howls
He rogers young owls
Which he keeps in an underground aviary.

That's the real thing. What's most important about limericks is that they be rude and scatological, but never truly vulgar. Words such as ——, ——, ——, and —— have no place in the proper limerick. The trench is precariously narrow between run-of-the-mill VFW smut and innocuous oddball pornography.

The limerick's appeal probably lies in its almost childishly simple scan. Ba-*bop*pa-da-*bop*pa-da-*bop*pa-da/ Ba-*bop*pa-da-*bop*pa-da-*bop*pa-da/ Ba-boppa-da-*ba*/ Ba-boppa-da-*ba*/ Ba-*bop*pa-da-*bop*pa-da-*bop*pa-da.* Almost childish, but even more, boyish. It's churlish young smartypants of whatever age who create and consume limericks. Doodling a limerick is how a lad misspends some hot Sunday afternoon after guzzling a pot of fresh limeade, bored with frying anthills under a magnifying glass and paying secret homage to womanhood.

* Some will argue that *this* scatlike abstraction should be considered the real thing. If we're limiting ourselves to modernist limericks, I'm inclined to agree, except that the third line seems excessively off-color, and the second "*bop*pa" in the last line is a bit precious.

There are non-pornographic limericks, to be sure. But certain restaurants serve meatless "hamburgers," and we don't eat those. Sheer whimsy can and should take an infinitude of metrical forms. But for berserk, high-toned depravity, you need the reliable old limerick. The versifiers may play around with nobler emotions, but for dirt, the conspicuous plain brown wrapper of limericks can't be beat.

BALLETS

Giselle is the real thing . . .
and as a fact of ballet history is second in significance only to
the ballerina Camargo's decision, around 1730, to shorten her
dress so that audiences might better ogle her *entrechat*.
Gas and strong toes made *Giselle* possible. Nineteen years
before *Giselle* was first danced at the Paris Opera, the owners
of the place installed a system of gas lighting onstage. The
misty luminescence thereby produced gave Romantic ballet
the means of becoming as ethereal in execution as in conception. Eighteen twenty-one—one year before Parisian audiences first witnessed this scenic gaseousness—is the date of the
earliest known drawing in which a dancer stands on tiptoe.
(Or *sur les pointes*, apparently deriving from the name of
fourteenth-century Alsatian nobleman Sir Lester Pwanh, the
legendary "Tiptoeing Lord," later to become King Lester the
Seemingly Tall.) For reasons modern podiatric scholars still
don't fully understand, the development of *sur les pointes* is
held to be crucially important, the premiere innovation of
Romantic ballet.* And it permitted Romantic ballet itself to

* Here in the U.S.A. we were amassing the first steamboat fleets
and gearing up for some serious manifest destinizing, and the French
come up with *tiptoes* as their major cultural payout? No wonder they
couldn't whip the Jerries.

flower, which was necessary before *Giselle* could become the apotheosis of the style. Which it did.

Part of *Giselle*'s Romance owes to what one critic saw as "the amazingly impetuous spontaneity with which the drama is developed," and to "its simplicity and clearness of plot." It's no wonder *Giselle* is the model of spontaneity and this is the neat thing: barely two weeks passed between the June afternoon when Théophile Gautier cribbed the idea for the ballet from a book of German folk legends—by his friend the poet Heinrich Heine—and the ballet's first public performance. Story, libretto, score, scenery, and rehearsals all perfectly polished in less time than it takes the modern writer to decide to buy a new typewriter ribbon.†

Giselle's plot is more than a little loony. Giselle is a pretty Rhineland peasant girl, not very bright, mad to dance at the slightest provocation, and purely in love with Albrecht, a duke. Albrecht has all along posed as a peasant and concealed from Giselle his engagement to the snobby princess. The deceptions are revealed to Giselle by a jealous suitor, whereupon she loses her naïve peasant-girl composure. She dies, and goes not to heaven but to the second act, where she's initiated into the sisterhood of the Wilis. The Wilis are the white-slipped ghosts of young virgins, all oddly passionate about dance, whose fate—being the land-based, non-singing cousins to the Sirens—is to lure young men into a fatal marathon waltz.

These sylphs begin to work their hyperkinetic ways with Albrecht, come to mourn his late lamented Giselle. He is

† Demographers have tendered a possible explanation for this unseemly lack of procrastination among nineteenth-century men of letters. In the years preceding the Second Republic, according to census figures of the time, there were in Paris 8.3 muses for every 1,000 inhabitants. This compares with a modern American Muse Ratio of only 2.1. (The French superabundance declined sharply by 1900, incidentally, due mainly to the emigration of the finest muses, enraged by the work demands imposed by the Symbolists and bored with the same old Montmartre hangouts. Most settled in Douglaston, Queens, where their descendants streak their hair and teach macramé.)

compelled by this unholy peer-group pressure to dance and dance in a frenetic *pas de dix ou quinze,* and yet as he slumps in tapped-out delirium, near death, dawn comes, the Wilis scat, and Albrecht—wiser, sadder—lives. Curtain. Applause.

Now the stories of ballets, like those in opera, are always unbelievably simple-minded. But the logical sense of the libretto is beside the point, since the very idea of romance implies a wonderful, colossal oversimplification. Romantic ballet should be *ballet,* not an Op-Ed page essay set to music. And we're proceeding here, of course, from the premise that the real ballet must be a Romantic one.

Giselle is the clear choice. But there are other contenders, and each of them incorporate five or six out of the following Six Essential Characteristics. (You may want to clip 'n' save this checklist, have it laminated, and keep it handy as a nifty wallet reference guide to the dance. Who knows when you might run into Baryshnikov and be at a loss for anything to say but "I hear there're a lot of homosexuals involved with ballet.")

1) The female lead is delicate, frail, and exquisitely beautiful, almost birdlike. Or even an actual bird (e.g., *Swan Lake*).

2) Somebody's soul is in torment.

3) Womanly wisdom wins out over masculine folly, this male foolishness taking the forms of philandering, the pursuit of illusory ideals or superficial sheen, misapprehending true love, and not being sexually attracted to large water fowl.

4) The music is music you couldn't possibly use for anything else, or shouldn't want to. *Giselle*'s score, by the pleasantly second-rate Adolphe Adam, is like an old sachet of blue satin, still fragrant but never very chic.

5) Love redeems the lead characters from stupidity, cupidity, and darkness.

6) Every fifteen minutes or so, the stage is mobbed by

happy peasants, waltzing, or grief-stricken peasants, creeping.

The only thing *Giselle* wants for is birdhood. But since the Wilis are sort of phantom hovercraft—the hems of their lingerie, according to legend, perpetually dewy—the avian requirement may be considered fulfilled. *Giselle* also is good and short.

Doggie style is the real thing . . .
which is not to say that it's more natural or liberated than the
meat-and-potatoes mode of carnal interface known as the
missionary position. But rear entry is the configuration that
summons up atavistic memories of rutting in cold caves, of
savagely taking the comely Cro-Magnon female after an anxious day spent stalking extinct mammals. Performing doggie style now and again also fulfills the modern demand
for variety. Orangutans and marmosets don't bone up on *Joy
of Sex* methods or use messy creams and oils—and there's a
reason for that—but neither do our jungle friends know that
what they're doing is magically sordid. We higher primates
have the best of both worlds.

Yet this is a new age. Maybe the day of hot tropical sex
groundhog fashion will fade, and doggie style cease to be its
quintessential kind. A prediction for the near future? I'd bet
that within a decade or two, the real thing among sexual positions will take a highly novel form: *both partners on the bottom.* Strike you as farfetched? Already we see, or at least hear
about, a sexual scramble to defer, to be ravished, to make
points on passivity. There's a post-feminist fad sweeping the
nation's bedrooms with the viscous inexorability of a coastal
mudslide.* "But both on the bottom? That's impossible!" In-

* Despite Freud and residual adolescence, it's hard to understand

convenient or uncomfortable, perhaps, but never impossible:
If they can land men on the moon, etc.

what all the sexual fuss is about. When you figure that the average man spends no more than nine hours during his whole life actually experiencing sexual climax, it seems we squander an excess of energy in this tormented connection. Cultivating dwarf shrubs is more satisfying to many, in the long run.

Richard II is the real thing . . .
because he and his reign embody nearly all the uneasiness intrinsic to the 900-year-old English monarchy. A quick and superficial summary will give you the idea:

1) Richard II ruled from 1377 to 1399, that juicy period in British history tucked right between the Middle Ages and the Renaissance. This is when pails of hungry leeches and non-prescription amulets were as slick as medical technology got. And Richard was the first English king to reign after the Black Death.

2) Richard died at thirty-three, after having assumed the throne when he was *ten*.

3) At the age of fourteen, Richard is supposed to have soberly faced down a mob of rebellious peasants who were murmuring threateningly and shaking hoes and rakes. This seems more convincing proof of royal fortitude than pulling swords from stones or marrying pleasant-looking naval officers called Philip.

4) Richard was murdered on the orders of his successor, in his successor's castle.

5) He popularized the handkerchief.

6) He was, until Warren Harding, the last of the Plantagenet line.

7) If we can trust the very famous playwright William Shakespeare, the sequel to Richard I was a good-hearted but incompetent chief.

GURUS

Guru Maharaj Ji is the real thing . . .
and I so designate him fully expecting a crack squad of jealous Moonies, all goony-eyed and dangerous, to descend on me at any moment. But we must stand resolute in our faith, the example of Sir Thomas More our beacon light. We mustn't be deterred by the threat of holy dismemberment at the hands of prostrate acid casualties. The truth is that the Reverend Sun Myung Moon can't hold a candle to the boy Messiah, and truth must be told.

The Scientology people are nearly as sinister as the Moonies, but at least they don't push founder L. Ron Hubbard as a demigod. Hubbard is the Howard Hughes of the field, a pseudoscientific grifter grown rich off the confused goofs who pay huge sums to take a series of primitive lie-detector tests. Moon, on the other hand, is an oriental Billy Sunday with an income of several millions, a newspaper, hotels, fascist underpinnings, and a battalion of steely shock troops who enslave lonely teenyboppers for fun.

Werner (*est*) Erhard (né Jack Rosenberg) is by comparison a razor-cut Jesus Christ whose miracles happen to take the form of turning whines into cash. Erhard's grossing $15 million a year, and one in a thousand Americans has been *ested*—about the same number arrested every year for aggravated assault. *Est* is an immaculate deception. If you were as cute and sincerely unpleasant as Werner, John Denver and Valerie Harper might sing your praises too. (Maybe nobody begrudged Dale Carnegie his success because he didn't wear cashmere or live in Malibu.)

There are so many more spiritual masters of note, almost all benign, and all of whose devotees sound like minor-market FM rock deejays. (A few actually sound like radios, static and all.) There's TM® and its Mahareshi, who since the Beatles and Mia Farrow has alchemized into the Ronald McDonald of his mass-market mantra concession. Then there are the Eastern salvation experts on the fringes of renown: the quiet and very tasteful Muktananda; Sri Swami Satchidananda, a solid blue-chip yogi; the oh-so-American Baba Ram Dass, Ph.D.; Sri Chimnoy, the amateur abstractionist from Queens, New York; Stephen Gaskin (it used to be simply "Stephen"), our home-grown spiritual Pied Piper who's now set up his own Holy Land in Kentucky; and Oscar Ichazo's vaporous Arica, once the sleek psychic cure-all to the carriage trade, now just this side of defunct.

There are the shaven, saffron-robed Hare Krishnas, those hyperkinetic exhibitionists who (like most American Christians, come to think of it) hang out on city streets, hold pot-luck dinners, and worship a dead guru.

Swami Vishnu Devananda is a lot of fun for avatar-watchers. His entire advertising campaign consists of an indignant debunking of TM. One feature of these ads is a chart which purports to show how TM's mantras are assigned solely on the basis of age: all eighteen-year-olds get one mantra, Devananda claims, all twenty-six-year-old meditators get another, and so on.* This broadside exposé is supposed to

* I, like so many others of our troubled generation who lay awake nights with the threat of the Bomb hanging over our heads, have practiced TM. Obedient truth-seeker to the end, I have never revealed my TM mantra to curious friends and loved ones. And although my mantra is on Devananda's list, it is *not* the one I should have been assigned according to my age at the time of initiation. Maybe I've been using the mantra of a forty-two-year-old all this time. Perhaps this at last is the explanation for my strange desire to discipline teen-agers, make mortgage payments, and paint rumpus rooms.

make TM practitioners slam palm against forehead and cry angrily, "Holy cow! All along I thought my mantra was picked especially for *me*. Boy, was I taken for a ride!" In any event, Devananda is pissed off. "PLEASE HAVE YOURSELF REINITIATED FREE OF CHARGE," his ad pleads, since "mispronunciation of Mantras may result in negative psychic reactions." (And in being sneered at by any Sanskrit scholar within earshot, he neglects to mention.)

To recite a complete Who's Who of gurus, masters, and spiritual handymen would require hours. You can explore the cosmos with Dhyani Phorner (who sounds suspiciously as though he used to be called "Dan Forner"), Gurudev Chitrabhanu, Gopi Krishna, Swami Rama, Sivananda Jayanthi, Shih-fu Sheng-Yen, Shri Ramamurti, Lama Norlha, and scores of other unpronounceably named Indians who think they're too good to eat sirloin. (Uh-oh: I suddenly feel the onset of negative psychic reactions.)

Maharaj Ji is *that kid*. Still stuck in the public mind at the point of his sudden notoriety, Guru Maharaj Ji (pronounced, without pause, like babytalk words for a desert hallucination: goo-mi*rage*-ee) is widely and incorrectly known as "The Fifteen-Year-Old Perfect Master." He's still Perfect, but the lad is over twenty-two now, married, with three kids. The kids are called Premlata, Hans, and Dayalata. Mrs. Ji used to be Marolyn Johnson and an airline stewardess. While her fellow stews were angling to become the wife of some cute marketing V.P. in the first-class cabin, Ms. Johnson hit on that prepossessing Indian fellow who is, by many accounts, God. Some girls have all the luck.

It would be beside the point to dissect the technical aspects of the Maharaj Ji discipline. There's a four-part meditation which purportedly delights all the senses save that of touch. (The *food* of the spheres? I guess so.) But meditation is meditation, and prayer is prayer. What these disciples (or *premies*) have is a living, breathing master dispensing joy and direction, and somehow keeping them from turning zombie.

Oh, and how he dispenses, especially at the bimonthly gatherings of the faithful around the world. In London not long ago, 'Maharaj Ji said this to his thousands of rapt communicants:

> And premies, a simple question: are we going to find out what it is to sit back and relax in the beautiful, beautiful, beautiful boat of Mercy, of Grace, and let it go? Or are we always going to be throwing up on the side of the boat? Even when you get sick riding on a boat, you want to give different things a try. . . . You try maybe five different things to prevent you from puking. What about in your real life? Because when you throw up on your real life, where do you end up? Okay, so there are a million books and a million concepts that can take place. *Endless* things. *Or*, you can become a ghost after you die, and you'll always hang around there, and you'll be able to do anything you want: get back at your boss, or do anything you want, and he won't see you. Right?

Not the straightforward eloquence of Ram Dass's best-selling *Be Here Now* (or even his more complex recent work, *Be Here as Soon As It's Convenient*), but Jesus himself wouldn't have sounded so great stumbling through English either. Maharaj Ji just needs a good editor; with a King James version of his teachings, outsiders might lie down and take notice.

But the man's lack of rhetorical aplomb doesn't hurt his standing with the ten thousand American followers. Indeed, the premies make no bones about the fact—*fact*, they say, not thin "belief"—that this squabby person is the word of God made fleshy, the contemporary edition of Christ, Buddha, Mohammed, and the rest of the A-list prophets.

The most obvious unbeliever's case against Maharaj Ji is the material opulence he enjoys. Come *on*, they scoff: a Malibu mansion, a Florida hideaway, a helicopter and a computer, the sports cars, the airplanes, Telex networks, sound studios and such, these baubles have no proper place in the life of a divine one. Sandals, poverty and hair-shirts are more reasonable holy togs.* *But if you knew that God was among us physically, today, wouldn't you want him afforded every conceivable luxury?* But why does the Lord of the Universe, reply the skeptics, need a Betamax? *He's just playing a joke on the world.* You're nuts, say the unconvinced masses. *That's what they said about Peter and Matthew and John,* riposte the unshakable worshipers. And so on, *ad nauseam.*

Faith is the bottom line. And Guru Maharaj Ji shepherds more people with more faith in him than any other guru on this sector of the planet. Is this overfed Indian joyrider —forsaken by his mother, brothers, and the media—is this the guy I'm really talking to when I say "Forgive me, God"? I know not what I do, but time will tell. In the meantime: Don't call us, He'll call you.

* I've always thought public TV's "Mr. Rogers" would make a good guru. He's so darn friendly and tranquil, he must know something about the meaning of existence that escapes the rest of us. Even parents wouldn't mind so much if their spaced-out progeny took spiritual marching orders from a fortyish gentleman with kind eyes who wears a cardigan and sneakers.

Richard Speck is the real thing . . .
but only a jot ahead of Charles (no relation to Walt) Whitman. It's surely the vision of Whitman which is the more dra-
matic now, in a dozen years' hindsight: a glint crouched on
the tip of a tower in Texas, hot blue skies blaring overhead, a
bundle of firearms and one devilish brain tumor his only
companions. Ghastly-but-true, mass murder is one of those
"only in America" phenomena which actually may be unique
to our simmering nation.

Richard Speck's murders were committed in the gritty
heartland—Chicago, also the home of the mad insulater John
Gacy—and that gives poor, hideous Richard a requisite Every-
man quality his fellows generally lack. Speck had no motive,
not even chimeric demons. He did his deed quickly, using a
knife, up close. The Tate and LaBianca murders were prima-
rily knifings—they used the whole range of flatware, in fact—
but Charles Manson himself usually wielded nothing deadlier
than a spooky stare. Wayne Henley—no relation to the Re-
gatta—certainly qualifies as a *mass* murderer, but the young-
homosexual-runaway angle gives that story an aberrant tilt, as
does Juan Corona's non-standard ethnic heritage in his murky
case.

Richard Speck brought Manifest Destiny home, brutally
dispatching eight young Filipino nurses. Nurses from any

nation might have struck a chord—the altruism, all that starched *white*—but that they were Southeast Asian immigrants smells predictable, almost pat. And Speck's prophetic (albeit understated) tattoo—"Born to Raise Hell," it says—proved that superficial first impressions ought not to be taken lightly.

It looked for a spell as if Manson had founded a new suburban subrubric: the Bizarre Hippie Cult Mass Murder. But those 1969 killings—which some experts have ascribed to the reckless combination of hallucinogens and ill breeding—turned out to be a fascinating exception, like most everything else that happened during the late 1960s. The true mass murderer remains a pock-marked little guy like Speck, the kind of sallow young man stunned neighbors describe to reporters as "a real loner . . . kinda odd sometimes, but seemed like an ordinary fella . . . stayed up late watching TV . . . didn't know him too well . . . he liked animals."

Today Speck lives at Stateville prison in Joliet, where he's been told he must spend the next four hundred years, at least. But with time off for good behavior, Speck could be a free man as early as 2094.

The Grateful Dead is the real thing . . .
as surely as they're atypical of the power-pop musical era now
in force. The Dead's rollicking untidiness, the self-indulgent
guitar solos that knew no bounds, the acid lassitude of it all!
Like no other group of plugged-in fantasts, the Grateful Dead
made it easy to muck around and *believe* (man). It was just
possible, sometimes, during a mesmerizing boogie, to forget
about that harsh light at the end of the sixties' tunnel of love.
Indeed, Jerry Garcia was probably the real thing of hippies,
period.

Unfortunately, these people are still making records, and
the music's saddening pap. I'm afraid we're going to have to
destroy their village in order to save it.

CHARLIE CHANS

Warner Oland was the real thing . . .
because and not in spite of the fact that he was thoroughly
occidental. Sloe-eyed, maybe, but as Caucasian as Sherlock
Holmes.

Six men played Charlie Chan in something like forty-nine
movies, but only in the first three (commercially so-so) *Chan*
films was Charlie an authentic Oriental: George Kuwa, Ka-
miyama Sojin, and E. L. Park, respectively.

Beginning with *Charlie Chan Carries On*, released ten
years before Pearl Harbor, Warner Oland, who was Scan-
dinavian, pretended to be inscrutable for the cameras, and he
did it in sixteen consecutive films over a seven-year period. It
killed him. Oland died at age fifty-eight in 1938.

The next player—first seen as *Charlie Chan in Honolulu*—
was Sidney Toler, probably a better actor than Oland and,
therefore, a worse Charlie Chan. Toler matched Oland's
pace, however, deliberately mispronouncing his "l"s and "r"s
in fully *twenty-five* editions. As it turned out, Toler's too was
an unintended lifetime franchise on the part. He, like his
predecessor, died the year following his last *Chan* performance. Mysterious, what?

If reincarnation is fact, I have no doubt that Warner
Oland resurfaced as a collie, transmogrified into one of history's several Lassies. Clawing the ground to indicate that little Timmy is trapped in a forest fire may not be Shakespeare,
but it sure beats purgatory.

John Davidson is the real thing . . .
and that goes some distance in explaining why the program's
ratings regularly plummet in the absence of Johnny, even
when his absences seemed only temporary.*
John Davidson is seldom *bad*. It may not take very long to
turn to the "CBS Late Movie" when "substituting for
Johnny tonight is John Davidson," but Davidson has never
provoked the wholesale rush to the channel selector that results from Ed or (especially) Doc announcing that David
Brenner, Roy Clark, Helen Reddy, or Bert Convy is the
night's replacement. Those are the nights when you gratefully
watch two hours of "Starsky and Hutch" reruns, and when
the rebroadcast of the "ABC Evening News," captioned for
the deaf, seems inviting.

On some nights, although one doesn't miss Johnny any
less, there's at least the prospect of an amusing substitute.
Steve Martin is horrible at being a "Tonight" host per se—
that is, at fulfilling the soothing, bread-and-butter Carson
functions—but it's sometimes a treat to stay up and watch

* I realize this whole question is no longer in momentary danger of
being rendered moot. But I feel it will be important for generations
yet unborn to know why their mommies and daddies sit and stare at
a blank television screen every night at 11:30, and why, when they
tell their parents it was "really hot today" the folks shout back: "How
—hot—was it?"

him anyway. George Carlin generally deserves a twenty-minute grace period, time enough to see if he's feeling nostalgic for 1970 and epidemic naughtiness. Carlin was once as exciting as Steve Martin, but he's perilously close to becoming the Mort Sahl of the 1980s. David Steinberg, who's now lapsed entirely into winsomeness, might have been the quintessential guest host in 1972. Bob Newhart is probably the most accurate all-around Johnny fill-in, but certainly not typical. Of all the Brash Young Hip Comedians, Robert Klein, though rarely thrilling any more, is the best guest host *qua* guest host. This new one, David Letterman, seems to have been experimentally bred for the guest host role and in fact, he is astonishingly good.

Who else? Della Reese? She tries, but no. McLean Stevenson doesn't deserve to live. John Denver has always been in way over his head as a "Tonight Show" host, and probably as a speaker of the English language. Burt Reynolds is entertaining, perfect as a guest, but too much of a good thing as host.

John Davidson is peppy, bland, cute, and sincere in just the right measure to seem as though he'd be good at it. But Davidson takes no risks. Even his age—thirty-seven—has the feel of a contrived arithmetical average, and his face is the protoplasmic expression of moderate Republicanism, in tan. He's congenitally prerecorded. With Davidson behind the desk, the line-up of guests assumes critical stature: if "John's guests tonight are Bobby Goldsboro, Martin Milner, Steve and Eydie, and animal biographer Rex Fuller," the scales are suddenly tipped and Davidson doesn't have a prayer of keeping his weary audience. Only a bundle of hysterical décolletage—some fibbertigibbet like Karen Black, with her potential for embarrassing psychodrama—or a truly funny rarity, like Albert Brooks, will keep knowing viewers tuned to a Johnny-less show.

Johnny Carson is an unassailably brilliant performer. This

isn't camp irony: with Johnny Carson, there are regular glimpses of perfection, no matter how grim the particular show. Carson is the crème de la crème; John Davidson is non-dairy whipped topping.

"Discretion is the better part of valor"
is the real thing . . .
though like all proverbs, this one has only the tiniest kernel of
truth. Here the proverb-maker—Shakespeare, one of the his-
tories—was being overdiscreet, for discretion is not just the
better *part* of valor; it is better than it. The imperial British
paid a bloody high price to learn this lesson. It's important
for all of us, even if some of us don't run the risk of losing a
colonial empire. And most people now, anyway, have long
since relinquished their colonial holdings (except for my
friend Roger, who still rules vast stretches of the Malay Pen-
insula).

But perhaps proverbs are altogether passé as an instruc-
tional mode. Pithy sayings don't always wash with today's
young people, since contemporary youth is acutely aware that
a penny saved is a penny debased by the inflationary spiral,
and that people who live in glass houses are living in relics of
an outmoded architectural fashion.

Even those of us not so jaded tire of proverbial inspiration.
If today is the first day of the rest of your life, that probably
doesn't bode well for the next thirty years. And old bromides
like "You have to spend money to make money" are open to
sad misinterpretation: the slow-witted eager beaver who thus
blows his life savings on pedicures and trips to Sea World
does not, as a rule, become a wealthy captain of industry.

It's past time that we updated and streamlined our whole notion of the proverb. My own suggestion is that we replace proverbs with *adverbs*. It's unorthodox, but take Ben Franklin's famous prescription, "A stitch in time saves nine." Saves nine *what?* It may be famous, but it's fuzzy and antique. Instead, taking the advice of that proverb to heart, we pare it down to its essential point: rather than a wordy, confusing sentence, we're left with the terse and to-the-point, "Efficiently." From proverb to simple adverb, like that. No more annoying little nouns or messy articles and prepositions.

So instead of the ponderous "Everyone's companion is no man's friend," we'd have simply the word "Intimately." Again: no serious loss of meaning, and five wasted words saved for later use elsewhere. Every proverb can be distilled to its essence with this system. We could finally dispense with the preachy "A penny saved is a penny earned," in favor of "Frugally." And "There are no atheists in foxholes" might be replaced by the clean and concise "Desperately," or elaborated somewhat to "Desperately, religiously."* At the very least, it would be more fun than metrics.

* The compression technique would also do away with unfair generalizations such as this one. Who are we to say that *all* foxes believe in God? To me, that seems like pretty slipshod anthropology.

Belgium is the real thing . . .
granted a few assumptions we'd best make clear right now.
The Soviet Union, of course, surely must be this planet's
most aggressively boring nation *in which to live.* (There is, to
be fair, the perverse thrill of repression: anticipating a twenty-
year stint in the *gulag* can't be without its own curious excitement.) Yet for the one-time tourist, it's fascinating to get a
firsthand look at the glum people with whom we are Most
Likely to Exchange Nuclear Salvos. Similarly, for us thrill-
seeking bourgeoisie, China would be a great sleep forward for
any longer than a month: a sort of subgum Canada with re-
educated landlords instead of pack dogs and gangs of four
filling in for baby seals. Canada itself—the trendy country-of-
choice for many connoisseurs of international tedium—has
the French of Quebec. To be Gallic is to be objectionable in
many ways, but *jejuneness* isn't French. As to the Third
World, with zanies like Zaire's Mobutu and Cambodia's Pol
Pot, boredom is just one more natural resource these hearts of
darkness lack.

The craw-sticker is that Belgium actually considers itself
one of us, a highly civilized country. Even if you've been
lucky enough to avoid the place, the monarch's name is a
tipoff: King Baudouin I. *Baudouin?* Are they serious? Maybe
the logic is that if they give their stolid little hierarch an

130

Arab name, everyone will mistake Belgium for an obscure, oil-rich sheikdom. Belgium, the poor man's Holland, is fond of surface attempts at cleaning up its international act. Like having the gall to join with the Netherlands and Luxembourg is something called the Benelux Union, a let's-blend-into-the-woodwork gesture by the Belgians, an unending embarrassment to the people of ne and lux.

It's worldwide consensus that Brussels is the least engaging capital on earth, a city whose principal claim to fame is the name it shares with nature's most ill-tasting vegetable. And to reside in this bustling crossroads of the mediocre, Belgians pay through their lumpish Flemish noses, Brussels being one of the most expensive cities anywhere. There is no Eiffel Tower or Statue of Liberty to symbolize Brussels. No, in Brussels is the Manneken Pis, a two-foot-high statue of a little boy urinating. (See? Flemish is easy: it's just vulgar English, misspelled.) The New York *Times*, in its wisdom, called the peeing statue "Brussels' most famous, or anyhow *most characteristic* tourist attraction." And as if it wasn't enough to try to spellbind tourists with a three-dimensional smutty joke, what visitors see in Pis Square is a fake, a copy of a copy of an original statue which no longer exists.

France has Nice, Germany Munich, and Japan the sylvan peace of Kyoto. Belgium has Antwerp. (It *had* Rubens, *et al.*, but I'm unwilling to let them rest, nay, sleep, on those laurels.)

Sugar beets are an important crop. Gear-teeth manufacturers, and deputy assistant under-ministers for dry goods export have Brussels as their Mecca. Does NATO excite you? Do you daydream about the Common Market? The country looks like northern Indiana. It's filled with white noise and steam.

Their pathetic excuse for a social problem is the bad blood between the Flemings and Walloons. And that's as good a measure as any: a place where the grievance of something called a "Walloon" is taken seriously is a place that deserves a yawn as its national anthem, a swatch of off-white chintz as its flag. If you think of the world as a global neighborhood, Belgium is the family who asks you over for an evening of old home movies and leftover cauliflower pudding.

FRENCH MOVIES

Jules and Jim is the real thing . . .
but this may constitute excessive charity toward an already self-satisfied nation. *Jules and Jim* is as good as they come—thrillingly oblique, small and pretty, sexual, almost funny, and serious with the slippery power of a great dream that makes you want to yowl. But we should disabuse ourselves of the idea that a French movie is *a priori* a great movie, that to be a Parisian with a secondhand Arriflex and a thirdhand idea is to be François Truffaut, or that subtitles are anything more than a cheapjack remedy for actors who refuse to speak a language everybody understands. Remember: the French think Jerry Lewis is a genius, and it's a fact that A *Man and a Woman* was very dumb (yet not so horrible as Godard's *Tout Va Bien*, the worst movie ever made north of the 30th parallel).

ILLEGAL DRUGS

LSD is the real thing . . .
and unlike any of the pastel array of soporifics—codeine and
the opiates, Miltown, Nembutal, Quaalude, Tuinal—it's perfectly okay to operate heavy machinery under its influence. In
fact, it's encouraged. You'd be amazed by the unearthly tricks
that can be accomplished with a big Caterpillar 'dozer when
the operator is an hour or two into an acid trip.

The government says that something like six million Americans have bid adieu to reality as we know it, via tiny doses of
lysergic acid diethylamide. It takes just a pinhead speck of
pure LSD to rewire the brain for hours. A ton of the stuff
would deprogram the neurons and synapses of every human
on earth for half a day (during which mass planetary trip everybody would probably spend their time laying dollar bills
end-to-end around the equator, and—wired to the proper grids
—powering cities the size of Dayton, Ohio).

LSD *feels* mighty illegal. The downer family is certainly
more dangerous. But drugs like Quaaludes do nothing more
than unleash one's natural propensity for stumbling, slur-
ring, slothful sex, and behaving stupidly in general. For heroin
users, the notion of illegality is pretty irrelevant. Marijuana
used to feel illegal, and that was a sizable part of its rhapsody.
But as soon as members of the First Family and U.S. senators
start doing anything, the thing swiftly loses its sweet out-

law luster. (It was all the rage when I was in college, for instance, to sit around a dimly lit dorm room and take payoffs from Korean lobbyists. Like marijuana it's still illegal, but no fun at all anymore.)

"Speed"—the little packages of distilled zest known variously as Dexedrine, Benzedrine, methamphetamine, and more—has replaced the Protestant ethic as the mainspring of capitalism. Employers: if you ever have an opening for a nightshift job whose duties entail making hundreds of meaningless lists, those lists thrown away, and new lists of those lists made again and again in an endless cycle, look no further. Hire a devoted user of amphetamine derivatives and you'll have yourself one fine employee. Not only doesn't speed feel illegal, the sensation borders on the dangerously ultra-legal, with some histrionic users yearning to dress up in California State Trooper uniforms and apprehend suspicious individuals.

Tooting cocaine feels no more illegal than making a stock-market killing from insiders' tips. Both are technically against the law, but *everyone* of substance and style does them both. Really, you loon: one does *not*, at this precious and sublime level, get *caught* by the *police*. How can a drug sniffed up by everybody richer and prettier and smarter than you be seriously *illegal?* I mean, *really*.

There isn't a microgram of *soigné* speakeasy charm in the LSD experience. You might begin an acid trip with this approach or with a rougher, death-defying version of it. But an hour later, every comfy anchor of druggie smugness is ripped away, shattered, and you're afloat in preternaturally raging seas. "Oh, Lord! I forgot. I *forgot!*" you yammer at yourself after the onset of the second trip, the third trip, the fourth and the *nth* trip. You'll always forget just how powerful this stuff is; that's the nature of the yeast.

Why do healthy, reasonable people still line up to swallow a substance so potentially nasty? For some, it's the chance to remain in the comfort and privacy of home yet still experience deep anxiety and disorientation. But even better, LSD permits a user to feel for a few hours that he is thinking and perceiving not unlike an artist thinks and perceives. Naturally, the drug doesn't do a whit of good for the artistry of one's *expression*, and this great tease has frustrated many thousands of twerps. Simple foolhardiness never goes out of style, though, and it's encouraging to hear that once again, great numbers of young people are tripping.

I guarantee this: responsible grownups, people in positions of any power at all, will never take LSD, not more than once. Presidents and tycoons and schoolteachers could (and probably do) regularly ingest all kinds of other drugs: coke, downers, smack, speed, any of it: and get along smoothly. A junkie President could check and balance Congress all right. A coked-up comptroller could still comptrol expertly. Millions of inordinately relaxed mothers and fathers sign report cards and pick up the kids from school on time. But with LSD, all bets are off. And all appointments, decisions, meetings, phone calls, friendly nods, courtesies, proprieties, the whole repertoire of normality. LSD must be the most subversive substance ever made.

Research Fellow #27885 in Harvard's zoology program
is the real thing.
There are many positions (especially at large universities
and places where there are more cathode ray tubes than ash-
trays) that very few of us are qualified to fill. It will probably
be some time, for instance, before you tender your resignation
as assistant cashier at Bob's Big Boy to become an Emeritus
Professor of Restoration Drama. My own temper and training
have left me unprepared to design software, sell hardware, or
model underwear. I have only a slight (and probably at bottom unwholesome) desire to be a trampoline instructor, or
for that matter to hold any job which most challengingly en-
tails promoting sensible safety habits. I'd be found out
quickly if I tried to function as the director of the Ohio State
Polymetrics Institute. We don't *want* to be swineherds, and
the job of "Beauty Tips" columnist for *The New York Review of Books* doesn't exist. I don't really have any idea what
"interface" means; thus, all but a couple of menial, anachro-
nistic jobs will elude me forever. Most of the world's population, being either overweight, physically handicapped, insane,
or into a Pleistocene lifestyle, is ill qualified for most of the
world's jobs.
But Harvard's Research Fellow #27885 is another matter:

no one you know and no one I know—for practical purposes no one at all—is qualified for it.

This isn't a slot that gets filled by placing a "Wanted: attractive guy or gal, good appearance & manners, for challenging but incomprehensible scientific job" in the classified section of *Grit*. No, what's run is the following description, reprinted in its entirety from *The Harvard Gazette*:

> Research Fellow. Req. 27885. MCZ. Establishes and maintains radioimmunoassay laboratory, and participates in active research program in behavioral endocrinology. Research animals include lizards, snakes, turtles, and fish. Minimum requirements: Ph.D. in reproductive endocrinology, and broad knowledge of reproductive endocrinology of lower and higher vertebrates required.

Now the behavioral endocrinology part is no real problem. Almost all of my friends are high school graduates and have a working knowledge of behavioral endocrinology, along with conversational French and the correct operation of cufflinks. And more and more young people are dabbling in lizards. But *reproductive* endocrinology is beyond us all, I'm afraid. And *radioimmunoassay?* Only a very clever visitor from the fifth dimension could handle that, and even he'd have trouble with the vertebrates.

St. Lawrence is the real thing . . .
and not only because St. Sebastian doesn't have an international seaway named after him. Lawrence got lucky in the draw: as the patron saint of curriers, which sounds just like *couriers*, it was natural that a waterway be named after him.

What is a saint? Someone whom we venerate and who's able to intercede in worldly matters. That may seem a pretty fair description of your grandfather, but I'll wager Grandpa didn't claim secret knowledge of the Trinity and start a religious order after getting wounded at Pamplona. And, conversely, St. Ignatius never lived in an Arizona retirement community.

Saints are also among the few definite residents of Heaven.

It's not in any of the rulebooks, but martyrdom is a big help in any well-planned campaign for canonization. The child saints were especially adroit at martyrdom: St. Agnes, beheaded for refusing to marry, or St. Vitus, martyred for dancing badly.

St. Patrick has certain built-in advantages as Ireland's patron saint. For centuries there's been a vocal field organization out making his case. The Irish are good at publicity. But that's just the trouble: St. Patrick is close to becoming a green St. Nicholas *sans* reindeer. (We often forget that clownish old Santa Claus was a real saint before his migration from ancient Turkey to the North Pole.) St. *Pat?* What other saints are called by palsy-walsy diminutives? The Jesuits don't pray to St. Iggy, you may be sure.

Most saints, too, were nuts, or so we'd have thought had we been John Q. Roman. Francis of Assisi is generally depicted preaching to birds, and he was known to call inanimate objects his "brothers and sisters." ("Howya doin', butter churn? Good to see you looking so well, wagon. Talked to Pop, our heavenly master, lately?") You *know* he'd be kept under heavy sedation today. (Of course, St. Francis did have his episodes of pragmatism: he came up with the precursor of today's fad diets, for instance. His *St. Francis' 40-Day Quick Weight Loss Plan* [also called *The Assisi Diet*] was a thirteenth-century bestseller, despite its frequent side effects of fatigue, dizzy spells, and stigmata.)

St. Lawrence didn't pull any cheap tricks—like St. Paul, who had milk flowing through his veins—but Lawrence's death was an unsurpassed classic. During one of the regular crackdowns on uppity Christians, Lawrence, then a papal bureaucrat, was ordered to surrender the church treasures to the state. Instead, he appeared at the government offices with a throng of poor people, widows, and orphans. Pointing to his scruffy mob, Lawrence announced, "*These* are the church's treasures." The Romans were not amused, and in a huff, killed him.

His execution by *roasting* took place on a giant barbecue. After some minutes of lying prone on the hot grill, Lawrence supposedly said to his executioners, "Turn me over, for that side is quite done." And the irrepressible Lawrence, cracking wise even at the end, was soon sainted.

"Video Village" is the real thing . . .
and why don't you tell 'em about it, Johnny Olsen?
In a minute. But frankly, just the name of the show was
the real pearl. Say it aloud: "Video Village." The alliteration
is nice, and the McLuhanian overtones are spectacular.
"Video Village," the show on which daytime TV audiences
first saw The Twist performed, sparkled like a showroom Cor-
vair. Yet during the first half of the Kennedy presidency, when
"Video Village" ran, its name was downright pedestrian.

Yes, the day of bewitching game-show *names* seems past.
Gone are the trail-blazing productions whose very mention
liven up a murky history of American television: there were
the Beckett Interrogative shows like "What Have You Got to
Lose?" and "Where Was I?" and the eloquent "Why?" Today
we have "The Match Game." Back then we had the febrile
pleasures of "Public Prosecutor," "Down You Go," "Juven-
ile Jury," "How's Your Mother-in-Law?" and "Brains and
Brawn." I wouldn't bet against the imminent rebirth of "The
Bible Story Game," if not on a network, then beamed across
America by a hookup of low-watt evangelicals. But, sadly, I'm
sure we've seen the last of game shows such as "It Pays to Be
Ignorant," perhaps the most felicitous program name in TV
annals.

Some students of the game show believe that the genre

reached its apogee during the last half of the 1950s. They say that it was when rightly frightened Americans were filling backyard bunkers with canned hash and geiger counters that the game show achieved critical mass. This was when Joyce Brothers won big bucks from Hal March on the infamous "$64,000 Question," and when the dark and greasy Van Doren man did the same, pawnlike, on "Twenty-one." Indeed, during this epoch "game show" was synonymous with "*quiz* show." It was then that personages no less legit than Mike Wallace and Clifton Fadiman buzzed about the game-show ghetto like a swarm of nervous fireflies.

Until the early 1960s, it was still the old radio format, dragged unchanged before TV cameras. The producers of television, for better or worse, still didn't understand their medium: the stage sets were bare-bones flats with about as much pizzazz as a Belgian accountant's office, and the contestants on programs like Groucho's sad "You Bet Your Life" were aw-shucksy and unhysterical.

With "Video Village" the game show finally tailored itself to television and three dimensions. "Video Village" featured a studio-sized game board, a sort of Brobdingnagian Monopoly set over which the players would giggle and scamper toward cash! and prizes! By this time the programs of screwball humiliation—"Beat the Clock" and "Truth or Consequences"—were sniggering along famously. The manic pop-art venality of "Video Village" was the finishing touch on the mold for decades of game shows to come. One natural and worthy spinoff of the program was the "game show home version," as in "All contestants will receive the deluxe '*home version*' of 'Video Village.'" And so henceforth we could watch the shows all day and play the slick boxed home versions all night.

The man who hosted "Video Village" was Monty Hall, the chattering smoothie who later made his name and money as half-owner and host of the wonderful "Let's Make a Deal." Can it be mere coincidence that Monty ("Video Village")

Hall and Marshall (global village) McLuhan are both Canadians of whom the serious intelligentsia disapproves?

Our historical analysis complete, it's impossible to change the channel now without describing a short-lived 1976 show called "The Neighbors." The name had no zip at all, but the producers probably understood that the rabid video Americana they'd unleashed couldn't nearly be conveyed in a couple of words. On each show appeared a different set of five overweight, overwrought women between thirty-five and forty-nine. The women were *actually neighbors* and ostensibly friends. One of them had been designated Contestant; the other four had each revealed to the producers, before the show, a couple of the Contestant's peccadilloes. Things like "Mary doesn't wear any underwear to the supermarket" or "Mary thinks she could have any man in the neighborhood" or "Mary bakes brownies at 4 A.M. in the nude." (I only understate the ritualistic shamelessness.) Then Mary, facing her smiling tormentors-for-a-day across a jazzed-up game-show barricade, would hear the accusations against her, one at a time. Each of Mary's neighbors had a half minute to convince her that she was the one whose particular defamation this was. A populist "To Tell the Truth," only cruel and intimate. Mary, in order to win her microwave trash compactor, had to successfully guess which friend was the true defamer. Real anger and genuine bile would spill out. After thirty minutes of betrayed confidences and animus all around, Mary invariably won the prize. The show's theme music rose up, and the camera would cut to a full shot of Mary surrounded by her pawing friends, all squealing their congratulations and luv. That really was "The Neighbors." I swear it.

DAYS OF THE WEEK

Thursday is the real thing.

Discovering the essence of dayhood is a search that has for centuries obsessed philosophers and working stiffs alike. But let's look calmly at each of the seven days—not to be confused with the Dwarfs or Deadly Sins of the same number—and see if we can't all agree that those ineffable qualities of a day aren't just a little more effable in Thursday than in any of the six others.

Friday: Friday doesn't exist objectively. It is the International Dateline of weekdays, an imaginary rule between the pleasant normalcy of Thursday and Saturday's desperate dream search. Friday, still mortally feared by the world's fish, is a heady, free-floating admixture of relief and anticipation, all wrapped in the tidy binding called "Friday" simply to prevent the week from spinning out of control. Without Friday to bridle our baser instincts, we might all become permanent weekend beasts, driving aimlessly until dawn and screaming "Kill Piggy! Kill Piggy!" over our CB radios.

Saturday: This is the best day, everyone knows, potentially a precious island of leisure and merriment. It is the real thing of *good* days of the week, surely, but not of twenty-four-hour periods in general. Saturday is a corny promise of street fairs and smoldering leaves and too many cold beers. The whole point of some weeks is to see that splendid promise fulfilled.

Sunday: Like it or not, there are a lot of Christians in the world. And since their Deity-of-choice idled on this day, and blessed it, we are expected to loaf piously as well. No one in his right mind this side of the Bosporus would argue that Sunday is *typical.* Only a profound pessimist (since all children, rightly, hate Sunday) or a giddy optimist (since no American except shopping-mall salesclerks has to work on Sunday) thinks of the Sabbath as the quintessential day.

Monday: As noted, children all over the world slide into depressive moods on Sunday, the nadir coming at about 7:30 P.M. in all time zones. Scientists have discovered that humans reach the pit of their weekly gloom *one hour later for each year past puberty.* So by age twenty, the typical person bottoms out emotionally at about 3 o'clock Monday morning. Extrapolating further, the average twenty-five-year-old—married, one child, working hard, apprehensive—finds himself feeling most suicidal shortly after 8:00 A.M. Monday. This progression continues apace—deepest depression one hour later for every year*—up to age thirty-five. (That's when Monday morning despair grows to encompass most of the week, or the lithium prescription is renewed, whichever comes first.) Moreover, Monday is like Sunday except that you have to work and nobody (except maybe your Aunt Maureen) goes to church.

Tuesday: Tuesday is a contender. But the day that the French call something like *merde* falls too early in the week to be considered fundamentally dayish. The waxing week may have

---

* There is a handy mnemonic device for remembering this fascinating human rule: just think of the well-known British saying, Devilish Donna Operates Her Lathe Frightfully Early, Yes?

gone well, it may have gone badly, but it's too early for a proper fix by Tuesday.

Wednesday: This is worse than Monday in its own way. If we could, we might all like to hold our breaths, squeeze our eyes shut and sprint through Wednesday. Wednesday is stuck way out in the middle of the week's expanse, past the point of no return but with the weekend still a dim promise of salvation. Lord knows why "Wednesday's child is loving and giving." I guess he has no other choice.

Thursday: This is the day. For starters, there's nothing inherently wrong with Thursday. That may seem slight cause for calling the fifth day the real thing. But every distinction from Pulitzers to Olympic medals has been awarded on no stronger grounds. And when you consider that a good two thirds of the other days do contain serious defects, being a not-bad day amounts to something after all. What does myth and legend teach us about Thursday? Well, it's "Thor's day" and we know that "Thursday's child works hard for a living." It's the day that makes blues singers oh, so sad. "Thursday is the cruelest month," of course, and Thursday is the day on which the Americans traditionally buy refrigerator-freezers. All rather inconclusive, I suppose. But then so is life itself.

Thursday is when the week comes bending around the final post at last, the jumpy fear of Monday's starting gate forgotten amid the galloping momentum of Thursday. By Thursday we're in the muddy thick of it at last. The finish line's in sight.

But since most of us are not racehorses—and since horses, even thoroughbreds, are slow to understand metaphor—we need a sharper argument for Thursday. It is, finally, the only day we truly have as our own, the day on which our week of personal bangs and whimpers accrue into palpable shape. We can look into the mirror of Thursday and see what we have made of ourselves.

ENEMIES

Most people in the world are the real thing. It used to be that you could tell friend from foe by training a cocked M-1 on the guy and asking who pitched the winning game of the 1938 World Series. Things aren't so nicely cut and dried anymore, not in post-Norman Rockwell America. These days you might have to ask who took the women's doubles at Forest Hills four years ago, and even some smart V.C. sapper could conceivably name the winner of the 1974 Pacific Hang-gliding Championships. Today the enemy is within and without, and somebody's opinion of, say, surprise Sunday morning attacks on Hawaiian naval bases, is no longer a foolproof criterion of trustworthiness. We need a subtler measure in these confusing times, and that measure—fully tested and approved for lay use—follows.

The exam is in two parts. First, ask the suspected enemy to declaim on his choice among four topics: he or she must demonstrate an instinctual fondness for 1) corn dogs, 2) jazz, 3) systems analysis, or 4) four-wheel-drive vehicles. A convincing performance on this section of the identity-check pretty well establishes one as a good American, or at least as a French person trying very, very hard. ("Oh, to eat zee corn *dog* while ah em driveeng mah Zheep, it is to be having zee good life*style*, no?") End of screening module one. Now on to the fine tuning. Begin with question 1, and follow the instructions.

1. In the event of a violent revolution in this country, which of the following groups would you prefer to see executed?
   a. low-born *sommeliers*
   b. people who tell you to lose weight and quit smoking
   c. adolescents, except cheerleaders
   d. household pets
   e. David Susskind, John Cage, Shelley Winters, Norman Podhoretz, Phyllis Schlafly, Tony Orlando, and all the cousins on your mother's side
   f. Julius and Ethel Rosenberg
   g. the Bee Gees
   h. certain members of the Los Angeles Police Department
   i. the inhabitants of Duluth, Minnesota
   j. landlords, capitalist-roaders, kulaks, Savak officials, Charles I, and the incorrigibly tan

(All answers except choices "d" and "i" are acceptable, especially "c" and "e.")

2. Would you rather spend a winter afternoon drinking sangria and listening to Edith Piaf records, or eating doughnuts and watching a Carole Lombard movie?

(The latter answer, of course, is the preferable one. If the subject gives an unauthorized answer—such as "sniffing nutmeg and reading old speeches by U Thant"—notify your superiors.)

3. Which of the following inventions was the most significant?
   a. power steering
   b. atonal music
   c. carbonation
   d. the bidet

(Answer "c" is right. A response of "b" is grounds for deportation to Amsterdam.)

4. Which is your favorite amendment to the Constitution?

(Acceptable answers include the first, third, sixth, thirteenth, and nineteenth. Persons choosing the sixteenth or twenty-sixth are to be detained and mercilessly snubbed.)

Instruct your detainee to complete the following statements as they apply to him:

5. "Heck, I'm not much. I guess you could say that I'm really just a plain old——."
   a. wood-butcher
   b. international outlaw, bent on the destruction of all Western democracies
   c. descendant of the Medici
   d. crypto-structuralist
   e. Algerian
6. "My idea of a sound investment is——."
   a. *okra*, pal, and plenty of it
   b. War Bonds
   c. an option on the motion picture rights to *Favorite Recipes of the Third Reich*
   d. East Asian orphans, sold short
   e. a very special little *dacha* about eighty K. east of Odessa

(For both questions, "a" is the acceptable answer, but even they raise ugly doubts about ultimate predilections.)

FABIANS

The popular fifties singing sensation was the real thing . . . largely because the lesser Fabians lacked the foresight to appear in the movies *Five Weeks in a Balloon* and *Ride the Wild Surf*. Many people nowadays are unaware that there was ever more than a single Fabian.

The singer Fabian—whose surname is Forte—is familiar today mainly to the habitués of The European Cafe Deluxe Dinner Theater in Ponca City, Oklahoma. But it was not so long ago that he and the other Fabians (Sidney Webb, George Bernard Shaw, and the rest) would gather round a warm fire in London, knock back a few sherries, and debate the merits of Bolshevism, Charles Fourier, and Annette Funicello.

The story goes that one September afternoon, Shaw had had quite enough of Fabian's eccentricities, fearful that the handsome youth's odd style would discredit the cause.

"I was shocked, friend," said Shaw to the lanky rock-and-roller, "when you began wearing that ludicrous leather jacket. My distress became severe when you commenced your *wailing* at the Society meetings—'Baby, baby, I dig your tan' *indeed!* But this new hairstyle," Shaw sneered, nodding at the lad's slick ducktail, "surprises less than it disgusts. Good God, man, and you call yourself a Fabian!"

"Hey, G.B., off my case, man!" replied the short-tempered

singer. "Just 'cause *my* idea of social utopia includes no algebra classes and free onion rings for everybody, you're always *buggin'* me. You watch, Georgie: someday I'll be *the* Fabian."

Except for infrequent talk-show appearances together, the two volatile men never spoke after this encounter.*

And as we know today, the twists and turns of history proved Fabian right. This boastful young hunk who finally achieved stardom singing "Lifeguard Love," "Tiger," and "Misbehavin' Shavian"—and who had more hit singles than Shaw, Wells, the Webbs, and the rest of the Fabians *combined*—this pop singer is without question the authentic Fabian. (He's also a *bunch* more fun on a date than your average British socialist.)

* During one such joint appearance, Fabian sang his rousing apology for the Soviet Communists—"It's Their Party and They'll Die If They Want To"—and an outraged Shaw stormed out of the auditorium.

SIMILES

"Like a woman" is the real thing . . .
especially when spoken aloud, in the appropriate Fernando
Lamas alto. "This city, it is like a *woman:* you must be strong
with her. But you can never know all her mysteries."

Plainly, there's more to it than merely affecting a husky
Continental-cum-Latino voice. There's an implied colon: *like
a woman* demands some elaboration, an explanation of just
how whatever it is is like a woman. There's endless fun to be
had concocting insights with the *like a woman* core, grotesquely piggish though they all may be.

We can look to existing *like a woman* proverbs galore. The
Iberians, not surprisingly, excel at this. "A calendar is like a
woman," goes one, "both are good only for a year." And
there's the famous gong-woman simile, which encourages regular striking of both. Not all are mean or anti-female: Shakespeare likened woman to a rose and to a fountain troubled.*

For sure it's the dumb, thick-headed *like a woman* lines
which most catch our fancy. The more spurious the analogy,
the better. And so it's the amateur usages that gleam so. Such
as:

* It has been argued that "like a woman" similes are inherently in-
valid, that, indeed, there is nothing like a dame—nothing in the world
—and that there's nothing you can name, that is anything like a dame.
I disagree.

A colander is like a woman: both are good only for rinsing vegetables and draining spaghetti.

The rain, it is like a woman: when captured in large iron drums it can be very useful.

Ah, this car, it is like a woman: the appealing options, they add much to her cost.

Yes, compadre, and the desert cactus is like a woman: the sweet nectar within is not so easily tapped.

My securities portfolio, it is like a woman: highly diversified with a particular emphasis on utilities and low price/earnings ratios.

The King James Version is the real thing . . .
and it's a shame Protestants don't excommunicate. Use of the
ugly Revised Standard Version should be a sin unpardonable
by any penance short of flagellation. And the still more prosaic versions—Howdy-Doody editions like the Good News Bible—are simply beyond the pale. It's Inquisition time again,
and the Billy Grahams are in for a big surprise.

The King James is a beautiful dumbfounding work. Yet
the Revised Standard is the Book in far too many homes, and
goes a long way in erasing the scant traces of sublimity and
power that remain in Christian religion. The Revised Standard is enough to make you start browsing through the Is-
lamic texts for purity's sake; you'll never find coloring-book
Korans.

There have been some interesting English Bibles aside
from the King James. Many otherwise pious folk always keep
handy a copy of the so-called Wicked Bible so that they may
be forgiven (seemingly, at least) a particular trespass. That
version, published in 1632, hardly after the King James
presses had stopped, includes an obliging translation of the
seventh commandment: *"Thou* shalt *commit adultery."*
Twenty years after that neat gaffe, another edition translated
a verse of I Corinthians as, "Know ye not that the *unright-
eous* shall inherit the Kingdom of God?" And thus we had
the birth of the do-it-yourself plenary indulgence.

(My apologies to the Vatican, but I couldn't in good conscience designate as the real thing the Vulgate, since nobody outside a five hundred-meter radius of the Sistine Chapel has heard of your St. Jerome's little pet project.* I sincerely hope it doesn't happen that our unfamiliarity breeds a contretemps. I mean I'm sure our respective agents could work out a suitable addendum for the Italian translation of—oh, darn, what would it be in Italian? *La Cosa di Realita?*

* I was particularly sympathetic owing to the exhausting labor I completed during 1973, when I was given a Guggenheim Fellowship to translate the Bible into pig Latin. Ough-thay I alk-way roo-thay the alley-vay ofay eth-day, and so on.

Bonnet, meaning the hood of a car, is the real thing . . . because to our bored American ears, happy-nostalgic words for *machines* are a thrill to hear. "Bonnet" fairly drips with country-lane perkiness. If nothing else, the British today serve as an optimistic premonition of our own national future, demonstrating—not least by their speech—that the citizenry of a washed-up, enervated nation needn't mope around, all sullen and nasty.

The British, of course, use scores of words unfamiliar to Americans. How many times have you heard a talk show explanation of the difference between "public schools" in England and America? I get jumpy if a month goes by without Anthony Newley or Jean Marsh telling Merv or Mike that "what you Yanks call a 'private school' we call '*public* school' in England." Apparently if that point wasn't regularly clarified on national television, we'd forget and transatlantic English would become unstuck.

And, Lord, the comic mileage these same talking heads eke out, year after year, from pretending to misunderstand the British usage of "fag." "No, Merv, you see we British call *cigarettes* 'fags.'" Smirk, giggle-giggle.

"So *you* might get into some *trouble* bumming *Marlboros* here on *Sunset Boulevard,* eh, Lord Clark?"

(And the same exchange can be toned up for higher-brow

audiences. Dick Cavett might ask the playwright Tom Stoppard to elaborate on Britons' use of the phrase "knock up," which means to awaken someone. ("Tom, could you tell the story," Dick would say, his disingenuous Yalie eyes atwinkle, "of the time in Paris when you knocked up Harold Pinter. Oh, no . . . what?" Smile. "I didn't mean . . ." Smirk.)

But even non-televised mortals use these alright-already Anglo-American calibrations as conversational gambits with new U.K. acquaintances: "I mean, like you spell 'color' and 'humor' with a 'u,' right? That's really weird. And I hear you call your front yard a 'garden.' I mean it's so different from what we do. Like you'd probably pull into a gas station and say 'Fill it up with 'petrol,' right, am I right?" And tube for subway, pram for baby carriage, telly for television, solicitor for lawyer, well-mannered for stuffy.

Bonnet is the real thing. Like "petrol" and "boot," bonnet refers to that American universal, the car: anyone can imagine himself talking cars with an Englishman. But "petrol" is too easily understood, for petroleum—if nothing else in the form of Vaseline's famous jelly—is known to the dimmest statesider. But bonnet? You have to *know* what it means. The alternative is to go on thinking that the English put little gingham hats on the fronts of their cars, tied around the fender with satin ribbons, which of course is nonsense. (It's the Norwegians who do that.)

"Look under the hood, woodjya?" is as flat and nononsense as Kansas. "Please release your bonnet, sir" sings. It's hobbit talk. "Bonnet" makes you want to give a wink and a cheery tip o' the hat to the fellow checking your oil, or maybe even play "Rule, Britannia!" on your car's horn and renounce your American citizenship then and there.

But beware of using "bonnet" yourself. Unless you've taken tea and marmite and popped over to Euston Station all your life, you're going to sound stupid. Memorize a guidebook glossary so you'll know what everybody's saying, but never, *never* drop "lorry" or "shed-yule" into your conversations with Britishers over there. *Don't* say, "Take me to hospital, quickly!" even in a genuine emergency; nothing excuses omission of "the." You'll risk coming off like the late-blooming imperialist who checks in at his London hotel and says to the concierge in his twangiest American: "Pip-pip, old chap! Can you inform me at which kicky Carnaby Street shop I could buy a miniskirt off the peg for my bird here?" The English dislike us enough already. How would you react if Alistair Cooke sidled up some afternoon down in Sears' hardware section and asked, "Hey, good buddy, do you all know where I can get me a used Winnebago, cheap? I'm looking to buy a real powerful sucker, you understand?" It's not for nothing, after all, that Johnny Cash doesn't host "Masterpiece Theater."

LIBERAL ISSUES

Handgun registration is the real thing . . .
and is an issue, too, about which I have very strong feelings.
But more on that later. The advocacy of a federal handgun
registration law is the *sine qua non* of late-model American
liberals. Even more aptly, it's one question on which liberals
are stuck solidly, solitarily out in the middle, the plaid-
jacketed right-wingers and the plaid-jacketed radicals in alli-
ance on each flank. Both the Birchers and the Guevaristes
ache for an unfettered personal weapons market simply to
protect themselves from each other, and maybe pick off a few
unarmed liberals for sport. (I've heard the NRA does a brisk
business selling life-sized targets with a silhouette of Tom
Wicker making a point emphatically.)

I'm in favor of the federal registration of guns, and not just
pistols and revolvers but rifles and shotguns too. *All weapons.*
I guess you could call me a liberal on this score. But I go a
step further: I believe guns should all be registered *to vote.*
Yes. We struggled in Selma and marched in Washington to
eliminate literacy tests and poll taxes. Simply because your
typical Winchester .22 hasn't the ability to sign his own
name or read *Fortune* magazine doesn't give us cause for de-
nying him the franchise. If an M-16 is old enough to go to
war, well then, I say he's old enough to vote, at least in local
elections.

Karl Lagerfeld is the real thing . . .
but not just because he's more or less French, male, celebrity-
seeking, and has the faint tang of moral decay hanging about
him. Halston, for example, lacks only Lagerfeld's European
parentage among these prerequisites. And if Karl Lagerfeld—
German-born and weaned just before we overran Omaha
Beach—can pretend to be a Louis XV Frenchman, why can't
a boy from Evansville, Indiana, named Roy Halston Frowick
be born to the artificially purple?

But even more, the man who serves to represent this high-
strung vocation must be someone whose attitudes toward
women are a trifle extremist. On one Parisian hand you have
Yves Saint-Laurent calling his dear, dear women friends
"Muses," and on the other you've rough-and-ready Claude
Montana saying, "I'm not really sure I like women at all."
Neither is what we'd ordinarily call well-adjusted.

Saint-Laurent, incidentally, as well as the Italians—Armani
and the Missonis—are too talented to merit real thing designation. Their clothes actually look good.

But what of the Americans? Geoffrey Beene has a genius
for creating understated fashions for the independently
wealthy working woman. But Beene is a southern intellectual,
a sensible artisan who husbands his privacy; no way is he a
Seventh Avenue figure for the eighties. James Galanos calls

himself the "last of the dinosaurs." It's unclear what Galanos means exactly. (Are newly evolved mammals eating his young? Is a glacial flow moving toward his studio?) But it may be connected with the dresses he trumps up. These cost between one and three thousand dollars apiece and hark back desperately to the musty Golden Age of fashion.

Calvin Klein may be a name loaded with solid off-the-rack chic, but his clothes are cheaply made, overpriced, and, for women with a trace of zaftig or modesty, uncomfortable.

Bill Blass is to clothing designers what Shana Alexander is to liberals: a boring cliché-monger who makes a career living out middlebrow expectations. Everyone but his peers takes Blass seriously. If he and his clothes are the last word in navy-blue elegance, so are the suites in Hilton Motor Lodges. Bill Blass belongs on an airplane.

Well-bred women who didn't used to shave their legs now buy Perry Ellis clothing. His is the androgynous hand-me-down look. Ralph Lauren outfits are textile reincarnations of public relations circulars; they're worn mainly by beautiful, gilt-edged harridans named Debbie Corngold who put lip gloss on their nipples and sharpen their high heels to a point. Diane von Furstenberg is the patroness of upwardly mobile shopgirls who haven't the wherewithal to be comfortable.

As noted, Halston fills the bill on all the high-profile incidentals. It's simply that his *clothes*—the bedrock of Halston's $100 million design empire—are uniformly ugly and unflattering, verging on the slatternly. His simply shaped, bright synthetics seem strongly influenced by Mme. Filene and her Basement school of couture. There are rumors that Halston grubstaked his early collections with first-prize money won in the 1962 Vincent Price Sound-Alike Contest.

In their favor is the fact that Mme. Lanvin, Jean Patou, and Mlle. Chanel are famous and French, but two out of the three are women and three out of three dead.

Kenzo, one of a kinky knot yearning to be thought the industry's *enfant terrible*, makes clothes in screaming Play-Doh colors, in shapes commodious enough to shoplift a Parsons table or two from Bloomingdale's. Christian Dior has posthumously capitulated to the trend of plastering initial logos everywhere, and the clothes are conceptually moth-eaten besides. Hubert de Givenchy designs for women who would prefer that sex be optional. Claude Montana's clothes are just the thing for brainsick agents who, on weekends, like to pretend they work for the SS instead of ICM, and insist on topnotch production values in their daydreams.

Karl Lagerfeld has led a peculiar life. "When I was *four*," he says, using my italics, "I asked my mother for a valet for my birthday. I wanted my clothes prepared so I could wear anything I wanted at any time . . . I was mad for dressing differently at least four times a day." He learned French after the war from a refugee who lived at his family's country castle outside Hamburg.

Lagerfeld's clothes are bizarre for the sake of *bizarrerie*. Elevator operator (or organ-grinder monkey) hats with chin straps in red patent leather and black suede, brooches with paste gems the size of Oklahoma hailstones, enormous veiled hats, Michelin-man jackets, and exploding evening dresses worn with sneakers. *C'est amusant, n'est-ce pas?*

Lagerfeld gave a big party in Paris a couple of falls ago. Forty-two hundred merry French wastrels showed, dressed variously as bishops, gondoliers, courtesans, wizards, clowns, fascists, Casanovas, nuns, nobles, naked angels, insects, and Venetian tourists. A few of the thrifty came as syphilitic socialites. The host wore a labor-intensive reproduction of an eighteenth-century taffeta gown; its manufacture required ten seamstresses working three days. Lagerfeld's Italian maggiordoma came dressed in a black funeral shroud, and balanced on her head was a fisherman's basket overflowing with dead pigeons. Four attendants dangled the festering halo over her as she danced.

When Karl Lagerfeld stumbled across his cobblestoned

courtyard at eight the next morning, enfeebled by long hours of compulsory gaiety, his surprised concierge exclaimed: "This is the way it should be. People who live in houses like this should dress like you, sir." At least until after the revolution, he did not add.

WRITERS

Ghostwriters are the real thing . . .
despite the attention lavished on authors of demonic Nazi
thrillers or last year's several definitive novels of women in crisis. Ghostwriters ply an unenviable trade: there are no talk-
show chats or envy-filled bars. Their task is pure profes-
sionalism in the worst sense: this pen for hire, indignities
willingly suffered. The best they can hope for is an eighteen-
point "as told to Bernard Ghostwriter" line nudged onto the
book jacket. Even this concession to truth-in-book-packaging
is a recent—and unusual—practice. More common is a buried
Acknowledgment on page *ix*: "and to John Doe, for his inval-
uable help in the preparation of this book." Now there are a
few almost corporeal ghostwriters: publishers seem happy to
promote the fact that some erstwhile movie idol wrote his
story "with Mickey Herskowitz," or that a permanent starlet's
memoirs are "as told to A. E. Hotchner." As in all merchan-
dising, it's thought that consumers will reach for a brand
name.*

* But these understated confessions of collaboration don't quite sat-
isfy. Why not "as tape-recorded, transcribed, and made more or less
coherent by Chris Chase," or "as outlined to Alvin Moscow by his
agent over lunch, who went ahead and, you know, jazzed it up and
fleshed it out, and made up things like that crazy 1953 lunch with
Orson Welles in Venice, 'cause he's the best in the business, really."

Ghostwriting is the neighborhood sport of Grub Street. The ghost sweats and smokes over a buzzing Selectric while the author-of-record lives the big fiction. Richard Nixon, for example, is listed as the "author" of *Six Crises*. But there was a seventh, undiscussed: that of the book's ghost, who for his uncanny ability to mimic Nixon's prose received passing mention in the big book's stonewalling acknowledgments.

But the wretches do ask for it, after all. It's hard to squeeze out sympathy for these expensive literary call-boys who sling ink to make the merely illustrious or licentious appear literate. They line up to scribble for employers whose only familiarity with an English clause is Santa, and who order up their memoirs in the same breath that they requisition a sincere look, a tweed jacket and a pipe for their back-cover photograph.

Performing a brittle, numbing piece of work for little money and less credit: such is the unfortunate lot of the ghostwriter, and, come to think of it, all but a tiny fraction of the world's workers.

At least the ghostwriter has the satisfaction of writing an entire work. Lesser hands in the creation of books haven't even that tinny consolation. Indeed, most famous writers maintain a large and secret support crew, seeming nobodies but without whom nary a bestseller would see print.

There are the fine-boned *punctuators*, for instance. The punctuator is a man or woman, generally the holder of a Master of Punctuation Arts degree, who pores over writers' rough drafts and inserts all the appropriate punctuation marks. If you ever have the chance to watch a professional punctuator at work, don't pass it up. It's a humbling pleasure to behold the self-assured skill with which an experienced punctuator lays down a flurry of periods, colons, commas, and hyphens over a writer's raw, unpunctuated work. For sheer tension nothing equals the punctuator's craft; nothing less than utter precision will do, and neatness counts. It's expected consequently that the profession will undergo increasing specialization. Already in Los Angeles the semicolon experts have organized a separate branch of the Punctuator's Guild, and in Boston a group of young radicals, all masters of the exclamation point, are lobbying for laws to require that every book include a certain quota of exclamation points or inter-robangs.

Less rarefied are the professional *stunt-writers*. Members of this unheralded elite are hired, often by a publisher, to write excessively dangerous passages that the superstar author dare not risk himself. You'd be astonished at the number of best-selling novels which have had their trickiest and superficially most impressive scenes written by some un-sung yeoman stunt writer.

Remember the part in *Love Story* when Oliver climbs into Jennie's deathbed? *Stunt-written*, every last word of it. How about the scene in *Rich Man, Poor Man* where Tommy torches the house of brother Rudy's cuckolder? All the care-fully executed work of a top stunt-writer. You think Irwin Shaw is going to endanger himself on a high-risk chunk of writing like that? James Joyce is by now the single acclaimed genius of twentieth-century English literature. But never ac-corded credit in any monograph is the pioneering stunt-writer who fashioned vast sections of Joyce's polyglot barrage. It wasn't only Joyce's consciousness that streamed. In fairness, Joyce did perform more of his own stuntwork than nearly all of the modern luminaries. And Joyce, it may now be told, handled many of the (uncredited) stunts in his friends' books, staying in perfect shape with a tough daily workout of thirty abstruse bilingual puns and two sets of twenty-five allu-sions. Misplaced pride gets the better of a few writers, such as Norman Mailer, and they insist on doing all their own stunts; all too often, it shows.

For all their meticulous planning, stunt-writers are occa-sionally hurt, sometimes badly. A. Sodio Greenwater was a fifty-three-year-old stunt-writer in great demand during the 1950s, accomplishing awesome feats in the work of Grace

Metalious and Nevil Shute, among others. In the autumn of 1959, during what should have been run-of-the-mill work on a famous writer's novel, Greenwater left one too many participles dangling and finally mixed a critical metaphor. His once-agile mind was left a twisted, shattered mockery of itself. Even with today's computerized thesauruses and pre-fabricated modular dialogue, stunt-writing remains a perilous enterprise.

But there are yet other, less grueling literary vocations for those content to lap up the crumbs of authorial fame and fortune. The U. S. Government, through the Books for Peace and Literature Stamps programs, is a ready channel for the surplus production of America's writers. And there's no greater satisfaction than providing a measure of sustenance for the prose-hungry peoples of Latin America and Appalachia.

On the lowest rung of the ladder hang the free-lancing panhandlers. We've all been stopped on some busy city thoroughfare by one of these ragged parasites, always with the same mumbled appeal: "Spare paragraph, man? Can you lend me a sentence fragment or two?" Caution is the watchword in dealing with one of these disgraceful supplicants, for as soon as you dig guiltily into your pocket for an unneeded chapter title, you're pegged as a sucker, and the panhandler will demand whole prefaces, polished manuscript pages, and more. A sorry business, yet some few have actually composed entire novellas from these begged bits and pieces and now live in East Hampton.

SPECIOUS HISTORICAL ANALOGIES

I know the national patter is thick with these, that they are a specialty of contemporary Western man, he simultaneously over- and badly educated. Fortunately, though, most such comparisons don't aspire to profundity, or even seriousness.

Still, several hundred essays appeared in the glossy press a few years ago, all featuring some variant on the idea that "you know, like, America today is just like Weimar Germany. The whole *deca*dence trip." I guess Kennedy was supposed to have been our Kaiser Bill, and some future ultra-Nixon our Hitler. Rampant cocainism, desperate money-love, Brooke Shields, ennui, and short hair, apparently, are the tipoffs that our times are epochal and important in the Weimar fashion. The people trafficking in this creepy, self-important nonsense were people who considered themselves well-versed in modern European history by virtue of having seen *Cabaret* three times and knowing that Proust's first name was not Ralph. In fact, the only significant links between Germany of the 1920s and America of the 1970s were lots of dancing and bad architecture. If history were going to repeat itself, it would surely do so more interestingly.

But the real thing is a different history-repeating-itself notion, and one that gives powerful credence to those sketchy reports of pandemic brain damage. This one is more common, more durable, less pleased with itself, and even dumber than the Weimar analogy. The real thing is the belief that *our corrupt, permissive societies are duplicates of fifth-century Rome, doomed to crumble and fall shortly.* The cretins to whom this seems plainly true also whisper about buried Kruggerand caches and think Walt Disney was probably some kind of covert One World propagandist.

Would that the present era were half so entertaining as those last, lost-our-lease-everything-must-go days of the Roman Empire. Roller Derby is just not a satisfying gladiatorial substitute, and while illegal aliens cause consternation, the Visigoths really meant business. Besides, there's scarcely any worthwhile plunder these days, and our imperial cities are effectively presacked.

FUNNY DISEASES

I'll be frank with you: most diseases aren't droll. (We can even invoke a proverb to illustrate this little truth: *In a tumor, no humor.*) Finding a genuinely funny disease is difficult, on the order of finding an interesting commercial banker, a sexy reader of *Saturday Review*, or a well-written textbook. But though the search is exhausting, it is not hopeless. Legionnaire Auxiliary Disease, for instance, is funny but unfortunately imaginary as of this writing.

Crepitus indux is the real thing. This is a non-fatal affliction, mostly—an important prerequisite in matters of medical amusement—and it doesn't last long. In cases of *crepitus indux*, the skin swells up alarmingly with air escaped from the lungs, enough so that the sufferer looks like a summer-stock *Elephant Man* but not sufficiently so to cause a physician any excitement.

So plainly the crepitus patient *looks* funny, but even better, he is the source of entertaining *sounds*. When squeezed smartly, the inflated flesh makes a crispy, crackling noise, as if the body were insulated with a thick layer of Rice Krispies. With the possible exception of narcolepsy, a better party-time novelty item hasn't been invented. "Yeast infection" and "thyroid condition" merely sound like funny diseases; the words themselves are punchlines. In fact, they are unattractive and tragic, respectively.

(Also worth noting in these inflationary times is the fact that *it costs not one red cent* to contract a serious case of crepitus. There aren't many bargains like that around anymore.)

INSECTS

At just about the same time you learn about copra, decimals, and Fort Sumter, a clean, sprightly filmstrip purports to tell you why we need insects. Until that moment, insects' existential utility has never been apparent to you. *We need these insects because they eat other insects* (BEEP) *And because birds, too, depend on insects for food.* This explanation must bewilder and depress even the most naturally beatific ten-year-old. Why do all these filthy, annoying little creatures exist, Ms. Ondracek? Well, Susie, so that other filthy, annoying little creatures can gobble them up. Is it any wonder grammar-school suicides are on the rise? And if some dissident youngster dares suggest DDTing the whole unattractive lower third of the ecosystem—have silverfish or grackles ever done you any good?—he is exiled to the Life Sciences Learning Resource Center to write "Save the whales" five hundred times.

Flying ants are the real thing. Ants don't even have the gumption to live alone, or in small families. No, they dwell in great, festering mobs, carrying grains of sand three times their own size back and forth, back and forth. Bees, at least, manufacture a product we can expropriate, and roaches give New Yorkers something to talk about between criminal rampages. Grasshoppers are competent fishbait and played a big part in the American frontier's famously character-building harshness. Spiders spin pretty (albeit derivative) *objets d'art,* and are good for making young siblings shriek.

Ants, however, do nothing but survive and annoy. Even among themselves they are quarrelsome and nasty. The monumental pointlessness of ants' lives is rivaled only by gnats and certain civil servants. Ants are by no one's reckoning "cute," and their miniature death throes makes killing them not worth the trouble, no more amusing than squishing a crumb of rye bread. The power of flight only gives ants a mobility to better bother us, their evolutionary superiors, and it's a power they deserve little and use poorly. Flying ants are like the ill-bred man who wins the lottery and spends his prize on a motorboat, lots of candy corn, and ugly Christmas decorations.

FURNITURE

Ottomans—footrests, that is, not ancient Turks—
are the real thing.

Did you know that the purchase of an ottoman has been conclusively established as one of the three indications of true adulthood? Eating raw onions and saving receipts for tax purposes are the other two.

Ugly, overpriced, and (most important of all) existing to provide only a superfluous kind of sedentary middle-aged comfort, ottomans are our civilization's purest embodiment of stasis and decay. Inelegantly upholstered stumps of wood and stuffing, they just *sit* there on the Herculon wall-to-wall, chunky symbols of a mean peasant majesty. Still, an ottoman is a good gift for the sloth who has everything, especially gout. Cats, too, are fond of the family ottoman as a perch on which to drowse and condescend.

Ottomans may be the last word in dull decadence, but there are a few other things that ought to be said about the furniture kingdom. For instance:

Denim upholstery is fine in halfway houses for emotionally troubled white teen-agers.

High Tech furnishings are indeed ahead of their time, but who wants to live amid an evocation of the Great Depression of 1991? In a High-Tech residential unit, it isn't possible (or advisable) to relax, and tender thoughts are improbable.

There is no word in Chinese for "credenza."

It is for a good reason that Chippendale waterbeds are hard to find.

Modular seating arrangements are the perfect furniture for a generation unwilling to make permanent decisions and committed to token displays of individuality.

Like people, a piece of furniture covered in leather is apt to fall in with the wrong crowd.

In a few communities, it is a misdemeanor to use "antique" as a verb.

If God had intended us to use driftwood as furniture, He would have created it in several handsome Decorator Boutique Colors.

Platform beds exist chiefly to ensure that monsters have nowhere to hide at night when you're asleep.

Outside of certain Eastern European cliques, cement furniture is in disfavor.

There is a fortune to be made reupholstering household pets in floral prints treated with Scotch-Guard.

Recliner chairs make you stupid.

When re-covering old furniture, it is probably best not to patronize a shop whose clientele consists mainly of circus clowns.

Until now, "settee" and "breakfast nook" have never been used in the same sentence.

EPILOGUE

Ron and Sheila muddled through a divorce, and Sheila never again returned to the lesbian steel mill. Ron pushed himself through a squalid series of affairs until he was crippled, two years later, in a motor-cross accident. Sheila thought it a suicide. "It was probably a suicide," she often said to friends.

Scooter marched off to Vietnam, where he was killed by a stray shell in April 1971, while on patrol outside Nha Trang.

Frances and Septimo married during their stay in Antigua, and on their wedding night learned the truth about T.J.

Everyone else had their dreams dashed cruelly or, like Sylvia, succumbed to the debilitating, unrelenting poignancy.

All but dear, sweet, generous Alice, who had learned her lesson at last. She would think twice before revealing family secrets again. *In Venice or anywhere else.*

If Tom Wolfe's overburdened conceit is still serviceable, we are now on the trailing cusp of the "Me Decade." This is, or was, the epoch when millions sued for inner peace at any price; when the simultaneously unattractive and precocious could begin to call itself New Wave; and during which most of us found a deep, new contentment simply in growing (or eating, or becoming) ordinary houseplants.

This final tad of exegesis is the book's Me chapter, Me in this case meaning you. This is your chapter. No longer are you obliged to skim along, nodding agreeably, overwhelmed by another's judgments of life's salient features. Now begins your solo flight, your chance to arbitrate and categorize and wring out the vital juices where only you can, in that fuzzy space allotted to you alone: your very own life. Excited?

"Everything is beautiful," promised the refrain of one popular song, "in its own way." I'll wager that rosy hook is cold comfort to all the hideously ill-favored Americans mucking through cruel lives. A money-losing fireworks stand across the town swamp from your sinking mobile home, with the wife slurping up ethyl alcohol and the baby in a safe-deposit box— this, for instance, is not beautiful. But in that silly Pangloss lyric there is an analogous truth: everything is a real thing in its own way. Your clothing, the way you eat peas, your son's mistress, your C-sharp, your parents, your natural parents,

Dave Clark Five songs you know by heart, your hopes, your dreams, your collection of scale-model porcelain rodents . . . every component of your cluttered but cozy personal universe has the makings of a real thing. The trick is to find (or invent) the appropriate category. After that it's a simple matter persuading yourself that, for example, your pet dog Brontë is the real thing among Stupid and Unruly Mutts in Danger of Abandonment. Or let statistical probabilities work for you. For example, ask yourself: *"Am I a Jew living in Wyoming?"* If the answer is yes, or even maybe, then simple odds make it comparatively likely that you—yes, *you*—are the real thing among our few Wyoming Jews.

It will probably be easiest for you to begin with people and artifacts on the periphery: your golf pro, your blacksmith, your heroin dealer, your wife's home town. You should have no dreadful emotional stake in ferreting out the classes and categories they each represent. Did the mother of your children happen to come of age in Shawnee Mission, Kansas? You're in luck, since the place announces itself as the compleat Wealthy Midwestern Suburb from Which There Is No Real Escape. Darien, Connecticut, the uneasy town where Mrs. You made her debut? Or was she impelled by fate's harsh caprice to spend her first seventeen years in Lafayette, Indiana? *No problem.* Each one of those urbanoid places is a real thing, and what's more, so is every town and city on earth. Every tiny, unremarkable facet of existence—arguably a real thing. From now on, the argument is your responsibility alone.

ACKNOWLEDGMENTS

In February of 1891, Henry James sat in his Paris rooms, waiting for Cubism to start and the Lost Generation to arrive. One day, mulling his notion for a "very short tale," James wrote in his journal that he "probably shall find that there is much more to be done with this than the compass will admit of. Make it tremendously succinct," he cautioned himself,

> with a very short pulse or rhythm—and the closest selection of detail—in other words *summarize* intensely. . . . It *should* be a little gem of bright, quick, vivid form.

The story was published the following spring. It was called "The Real Thing." You can look it up.

This is certainly not to suggest Henry James as a benchmark for the book you've just finished. That way lies lunacy. No, even though I have (as did James) a social scientist for a sibling, and though I've spent time at Harvard and in London, and despite even the critical consensus that themes of disillusionment are prominent in my later fictions, I make no claims of Jamesian excellence.

In fact, the book's title wasn't my idea at all. I expect I would have chosen a title that had never been used before, at least not by a writer of such intimidating stature. Maybe I'm naïve, but I like to think *The Real Thing* was not selected as a constant, cruel reminder of my own insufficiency. I like to think that the muffled snickers, sidelong glances, and whispers that attend my visits to the publisher aren't the result of some elaborate practical joke that everyone gets but me.

Well into the manuscript and convinced finally that the corporate choice of title was unfortunate coincidence and nothing more, I was reminded that the great editor Max Perkins routinely encouraged Fitzgerald, Hemingway, and Wolfe to strive for "the real thing" in their work. Yet even then I vowed once more to ignore these heavy burdens of the past, for perseverance is my middle name. (Actually, *Perserveransky* was my maternal grandfather's family name in the Old Country, and so my rightful middle name. But as was the case with so many fleeing the hated *knishes* and *pogroms*, an impatient immigration officer took it upon himself to Americanize us.)

Now that my labors are done, the only reward I desire is your interest and amusement. Your respect, honestly acquired, is a precious commodity. It could never be equaled by a seven-figure paperback sale or some lucrative auction of movie rights. However, if each of you could arrange for your bookkeepers to forward me quarterly statements specifying the net respect I've earned during the preceding fiscal year, I'd be very grateful.

Speaking of gratitude, I owe a substantial amount to many people for their advice and assistance. For their offhand notions and factual shards, I'm indebted to Donald Doe, Jim Downey, Stephen Graham, Margaret Holmes, Bob Levine, Ruth Liebmann, Mark Magowan, Ralph Martin, and Stuart Thorson.

Larry O'Donnell was encouraging at several anxious junctures; my family read early snatches of the manuscript and helped more than they know by their various reactions, especially my parents, who laughed and weren't put out or off; and Eric Rayman gave sober counsel.

Holly Brubach's research was excessively good, far more than mere fact-gathering. She deserves special praise for several of the longer chapters.

Strat Sherman was affectionate and wise in all his editorial suggestions; his precise enthusiasms were a boon more than once. Mark O'Donnell was promiscuous, as always, with the favors of his remarkable mind. (Specifically, we collaborated on an earlier, smaller incarnation of the "Quizzes" chapter.)

Jeffry Culbreth worked wonders with splattered drafts and grumpy silences. At Doubleday, Hugh O'Neill suffered my elaborate panics, and his good sense was essential; Sam Vaughan may truly be the last gentleman.

Anne Kreamer will be repaid, somehow, for her forbearance, love and (not least) her sublime textual nudges.

And Gene Shalit, whose generosity in all matters is unequaled, was a splendid godfather. Without him, together with the officers and men of the United States Air Force, this book wouldn't have been plausible.